# On Writing and Publishing Your Book:

## A How-To Guide

By

Joe Chianakas

# Dedication

This is for all the dreamers out there. Is there anything greater than a dream?

Well, maybe a dream accomplished. Let's see if we can do that together.

This book is entirely self-published, simply to model what all is possible.

Cover photo by Apartment Two Photography and edited by Drake Sweeney. For photo inquiries, go to drake.format.com.

# Table of Contents

# 1
# Introduction

The question I get the most at every book signing and event I've done over the last several years is this: How do you publish a book? Teenagers ask me who love writing short stories. Retired folks, who want to write that novel or pen a memoir, ask the same thing. It's a popular question.

Five years after publishing my first novel, I decided to sit down and write a how-to guide on the subject. I've done seminars and lectures and hundreds of presentations, but nothing beats having a written guide to encourage you every step of the way.

Let's make a rule right now about getting published. I want you to follow this rule no matter what.

**Never pay someone to publish you.**

"But, what if it's a publisher who says the money is for basic expenses like cover design and press releases?"

**NO**.

"But, what if they believe in me and they say I'm paying for a premium level to be featured above other authors?"

**NO**.

"But . . ."

**NO buts.** There are vanity publishers who will try and make money from you the moment you Google how to be a published author. They're paying for ads. They'll look amazing and they'll promise you publication.

And they're scam artists.

You can do this yourself. You can save money, and keep your dreams realistic. And if you do want to shoot for the stars—agents and big publishers—I will point you in the right direction for that, too. But please, one last time for the people in the back—never accept a publishing deal from a publisher that requires you to pay them. Yes, if you self-publish, you may pay out-of-pocket for an editor, for cover art, and some other small expenses. Don't misunderstand me. Self-publishing in that capacity may cost you a few hundred bucks. But that's it, and there are scam artists offering you the dream of a best-selling author for the "small" price of a few thousand dollars. Run from those people, put them in a horror novel instead, and let them die.

So, why listen to me?

Also, sure, there are great books on writing by Stephen King and authors whose names are recognized around the world. Those authors are insanely talented and/or amazingly lucky.

I don't consider myself insanely talented or amazingly lucky. I'm a little of both. What you need to really succeed in this industry: either a lot of talent and a little luck, or a little talent and a lot of luck. Keep that in mind. I'm still working on both my talent and my luck!

I'm qualified and interested in helping writers because I have experience in the three main areas of publishing. I've gone the indie publishing route and worked with a small publisher. I've self-published books entirely on my own. And—after a lot of hard work and some luck—I managed to land a literary agent years after my first book published. My goal is to explore all three of these avenues with you. We'll talk about getting an agent and what the pros and cons of that may be. We'll discuss submitting directly to small publishers without an agent. And we'll explore self-publishing options.

All three of these options are great, and there should not be any sense of superiority when it comes to having an agent over self-publishing. It's going to come down to your own personal goals, and we'll explore that in more detail later in this book.

My full-time job is that of an educator. I taught English at a high school for ten years. Since 2011, I've been a full-time professor of communication at the college level. My goal has always been to teach. It brings me even more joy than writing. So, when I realized that I had worked with an indie publisher, and with an agent, and with self-publishing, I discovered that I have the experience in all three areas here to help out others. I don't think someone like Stephen King fully understands what a purely self-published writer deals with. I also don't think someone who has never worked with an agent should give you advice about how/if to get an agent. The balance of all of these is what makes me qualified.

When I first wrote a book that I thought had the potential to be published, I had no idea what to do. One writing tip that I've always found useful is to write the kind of book that you would want to read.

So, this book is for everyone out there who wants to finish their own story and publish it. I'll do my best to give you good advice.

Also, I encourage you to write in this book—what questions do you have? What can be clarified? What else do you want to know? This is my first edition, and I decided to do this for a series of upcoming workshops in 2020. I wrote 100 pages in just about two weeks' time. I am sure you will have more questions. I would welcome those, as my plan is to update this book and create additional editions, so that I am as helpful as possible.

Let's begin.

# 2
# Getting Started: Agents and Indie Publishers

Many people want a traditional publisher or agent so that they do NOT have to do all of this work themselves. Writers just like to write, right? ☺

The other advantage is that you should be able to reach more people. There are pros and cons that we could discuss forever, but the choice of how you publish is always yours.

BEFORE you even consider querying an agent, have a completed manuscript, fully edited, 110% ready to go. Never query unless you are 110% ready to publish.

Let's talk pros and cons, and then I'll give you a checklist to follow, depending on what you choose to do.

PROS AND CONS OF AGENTS

The pro of agents is that they can query publishers and editors that you can't. Lots of small publishers will accept queries from authors without agents, but the big publishers definitely don't. So, if your dream is to be on every bookshelf in every bookstore in the country, your best shot is to have an agent.

In addition, they will have access to publishers of which you would otherwise know nothing about. Good agents are constantly networking with editors and publishers, so they should know the ones who are most likely to connect with your particular book. They are working on building relationships with editors.

Furthermore, they will often act as an editor—some very thoroughly, some just with general critiques. But either way, getting an agent's perspective would be quite valuable. They are the ones who know how to sell your book, after all.

But there are cons, too. The first is that getting an agent is difficult and time-consuming. Many agents take months to reply to a query and then may take months more before reading your full manuscript. It's a safe bet to say it would likely take you about a year to land an agent, so you have to be patient.

IF you get an agent—and don't be depressed if you don't, it's a very competitive, subjective, and picky industry—there are cons to consider. Agents will take a cut of your royalties, but they only get paid if you get paid. You likely will be contracted to them for a year, so you do give up rights to self-publish or query others for the work they represent.

Plus, it's very possible they will never sell your work. Having an agent is not a guarantee. They may come back to you with rejections, and then you start all over again. Or they may sell your book to a small publisher, which you could have done on your own. Then again, that small publisher may value an agent's submission more than an individual author's.

So, what should you do?

My advice—as long as you are willing to be patient and have the time—is to start by querying agents. Even if you don't get one, you'll learn more as you try.

What can you learn?

Well, you should constantly revise your query letter. Keep track of any requests you get for full manuscripts. Those query letters caught their attention, so you know you have a good pitch. Keep revising your pitch until you get a full manuscript request. This pitch/this query will eventually morph into your back-of-the-book blurb, too—and that's a great perk.

If your full manuscript gets rejected, ask for feedback. Many don't have time, and they will politely tell you it's purely subjective. But some will, and you can then learn from that. Based on any agent feedback, you can revise your manuscript.

If a year goes by and you never signed with an agent, at least your pitch (which becomes your back-of-the-book blurb) and your manuscript will have improved, right? That's a pro within the con!

Let me next give you some step-by-step suggestions for querying agents.

QUERYING AGENTS

_____ 1. Research agents that represent the kind of writing you do.

TIPS: I look up the agents who represent my favorite authors in the same genre I am writing. Those are always my dream agents! But they can be difficult. It may be best to look at new agents within the agency that those veteran agents work. Also, do a Google search for "*Writer's Digest* new agent alert." They post the newest agents on the web, and those are often ideal places to start.

_____ 2. Personalize your query letters to them. Pay attention to their requirements for submission. Never send generic form letters to lots of agents. (I included a sample query in chapter 5.)

_____ 3. Develop an organizational system to keep track of who you have sent queries to, how long they take to respond (if they respond), and if they said yes or no. I start by using a notebook and transfer my notes to an Excel spreadsheet.

_____ 4. If they say no, politely ask for some feedback. Any advice helps, but please never get defensive or react negatively. Even through rejections, you are building a reputation.

_____ 5. If they say yes, research who they have represented and their success. Ask for references. If it seems good, congrats and go for it!

_____ 6. Pick up a *Writer's Guide to Literary Agents* text. This is a great resource to have on your shelf as you research new agents.

_____ 7. Work on new projects during this process. It can take a long time to hear back from agents. You might as well be working on something new.


INDIE PUBLISHERS

A different way to go about getting published, and a great option for new authors, is to find indie publishers. You typically don't need an agent for indie pubs. These are small teams—usually an editor or two, a cover designer, a marketer, and more—who work together to publish and promote your work.

It's a great way to learn. My advice: if you go through indie publishers, research who they have published and reach out to those authors to see if they have had a good experience. Make sure you do get to work with a professional editor and cover designer and that – if the publisher takes a cut of your royalties—you do NOT have to pay for these services on your own. They should pay for that.

Where should you look for publishers? You can always go a Google search, and often the books on literary agents will also include sections on publishers to which you can directly query.

But a great resource is www.publishersweekly.com. *Publisher's Weekly* posts the latest announcements on publishing deals. When you see that a publisher has picked up a book, research that publisher. There are hundreds of small publishers, and they may accept direct submissions from you without an agent.

Research the submission guidelines on the publishers you find. You will submit to them in the same fashion you submit to an agent—a query, a sample, and often a synopsis.

The pro: You won't lose any commission to an agent if you score a publisher on your own. You will have a team who works with you on editing, cover design, formatting, marketing, and more.

And you should never pay for this, by the way! That's why the publisher will take a cut of your royalties.

The con: Like getting an agent, it can take just a long and be as difficult to find a publisher. There's no guarantee your book will sell lots of copies just because you have one. Often, the marketing is still up to you. We'll talk about marketing in chapter seventeen. You also give up some control, and you may not get the final decision on cover art or certain editing aspects.

Still, if I have the time and patience, this is my second choice. First, I try to find an agent. I would give yourself a year. If that doesn't work out, then spend a year researching smaller publishers and submitting work directly to them. Having a team to support you and teach you is invaluable. Even if later in your career you decide you can do just as well on your own as a self-published author, or if you prefer the freedom and don't have the patience, you again have gained a lot of knowledge about the industry. There's no better way to learn than to research what agents and publishers are looking for. It will help you come up with new ideas for books. It will help you revise your own material.

If after one year of searching for agents and one year of searching for publishers do not result in any contracts, do not get depressed. It's disappointing, of course. But remember that all art is subjective.

There are countless stories of authors who have been rejected. JK Rowling's first *Harry Potter* manuscript was famously rejected over a dozen times! So what if you take two years to research and submit to various parties within this industry? During that time, I would hope you are working on new material, too. Maybe you need to build your own audience. Maybe you need to show everyone that you can do it on your own—that you can be successful. Maybe that's exactly the motivation you need—a year or two of rejections and growth to find the motivation and build the confidence you need to just do it all on your own.

Two years of research, two years of learning, two years of working on new material: I'd say you are most definitely now ready to self-publish. I'm going to walk you through that, too.

I can imagine some reading this think that two years is two years too long. If that's the case, then you can always jump right to self-publishing. Once again, the choice is always yours. You may have your own reasons for not wanting to wait a year or two, and that's fine.

AUTHORS.ME

Another resource for your to use is the website, authors.me. This is a submission site that helps match you with appropriate agents and publishers.

Authors.me is a website that reminds me of LinkedIn but for writers. You create a profile, upload some work, and it matches you with publishers and agents! This is a new-ish way of submitting. I've played with it only briefly, but from what I could gather, it was legit. Still, always do your homework and research the agents and publishers that request more information from you.

Check it out: https://www.authors.me/

Authors.me may help speed up the pitching process. There's also one other way to help find agents and publishers: let's consider attending a pitch party!

# 3
# Pitch Parties

One of the coolest ways to find new agents and indie publishers today is on Twitter. At least a few times a year, there are pitch parties where you can tweet about your 100% COMPLETED AND EDITED work, using a special hashtag. If you get favorited, research the person who liked your tweet. Those are agents and publishers actively seeking new clients. Research carefully, though. Anyone can like a tweet, so do your homework.

Here are a couple of pitch parties to research.

_____ #pitmad Remember, to participate, you must have a completed manuscript ready to publish! See https://pitchwars.org/pitmad/

According to that website, #pitmad occurs quarterly. So, if you miss one, you can wait a few months and there will be another chance. Plus, this could be a good learning opportunity for you while you work on your book. I would recommend that you start a Twitter account, research #pitmad, and at least view the tweets that day by following the hashtag. They will give you good ideas for pitching your book. In addition, you may be able to learn more about agents and publishers. Just because you don't participate or don't get a tweet favorited doesn't mean that you can't contact the participating agents and publishers on your own. Their participation just goes to show that they are looking for new clients and manuscripts!

_____ At the time of this writing, there are so many new pitch parties, that they are now organized here: https://iwriterly.com/pitch-contest-calendar/ I would explore that site and look for events that match your genre and interest.

Some worth highlighting:

#SFFpit is for science-fiction and fantasy authors

#DVpit is a special pitching party for diverse authors or authors of marginalized voices.

_____ Also, research "Twitter Pitch Parties for Authors" on Google to learn and find more. It's safe to say that some previous pitch parties may no longer be happening, but that new ones will come about.

## TWITTER

Of course, if you're going to use Twitter to pitch your book, then you should start building a platform there too. It's a good way to network with other writers and learn from each other.

_____ Build a writing following and learn more through Twitter.

_____ Browse hashtags #amwriting and #writingcommunity

_____ Find authors that seem to do what you want to do—how are they publishing? Look for their specific publishers and agents. This is another way to research opportunities.

We will talk more about Twitter in chapter seventeen's marketing section.

# 4
# Tips for Finding Agents

In this book, we jumped right into finding agents and publishers, as that's the dream for most of us. I will be talking about the writing process in later chapters, but now's a good time to remind you of the most important part before even beginning your search for agents and publishers.

Do you have a manuscript that is 110% ready to submit?

At the very least, I would make sure you have revised your manuscript three times, and that's the bare minimum. (In my research, most agents will tell you to revise ten times or more as a bare minimum—no joke!)

When you revise, that means you detach from it for a few weeks, then re-read it, then edit and revise your writing each time you go back through it. The term "first draft" exists for a reason, and no one should ever dare consider submitting their first draft to anyone, and that includes self-publishing.

One of these revisions, at least one but the more the better, needs to have someone else's eyes review it. Not just for typos, but for general feedback.

Then before you submit, run your manuscript through a good grammar and spelling checker. I recommend Grammarly. There's a free web version where you can copy and paste sections of your book, and it will help you eliminate typos and errors.

After several revisions—including help by other readers— and a thorough check for grammatical errors: Then you can consider submissions. Focus on the writing first, okay?

## Some tips for finding agents and publishers

_____ 1. Be ready to be patient. This process could take a long time (at least a year).

_____ 2. Work on your writing—revise, revise, revise. If you get rejections, consider what you can do to improve. I'm sure you took my advice above and already had several revisions before you submitted, but guess what? That may not have been enough. If you get several rejections, you may need several more revisions.

_____ 3. Self-publishing and indie publishing are options, if this becomes too frustrating or disheartening.

## How to find agents

_____ 1. Shooting for the stars? Research who is on the bestselling lists in your genre. Then do a Google search to see who that author's agent is. Learn about their agency. You can query that agent directly, or consider querying a more junior agent at that agency. Newer agents may be more accepting of newer authors.

_____ 2. Google "*Writer's Digest* new agents." This is a great way to find those who are actively building their client's lists.

_____ 3. Get a *Literary Guide to Agents* book.

_____ 4. Upload your query to authors.me on the web!

_____ 5. Review chapter two for more information on this.

## Researching agents

Thanks to the internet, we live in a world where anyone can say anything. Do your homework and research on the agents you submit to, and especially research any agents and publishers that offer you a deal. Things to look for:

Who do they represent? Ask for references. Talk to those authors. Are they selling books? Look them up on Amazon and Barnes & Noble. Are they published? What are their sales ranks?

If their newest authors' sales ranks are 100,000 or higher on Amazon, then you may seriously consider self-publishing or someone else. A sales rank between 100,000- 1,000,000 means that the author likely is selling only a few books a month.

Anyone consistently below 100,000 means they have decent, regular sales. Under 25,000? That's a great sign.

Sales ranks change a few times a day, so don't be disheartened if the authors they represent aren't great. Plus, there are so many factors involved. If a book has been out for a year or more, it's probably not selling a lot. I look for those who had a release within the last month, which isn't always easy to find. But if an agent or publisher's newest authors have high sales ranks, then you should feel confident moving forward. If they have low sales ranks, there could be lots of other reasons for that, too. Use your best judgment when making a decision.

Other questions to ask your agents:

What all do they represent (foreign rights, movie rights, audio)? Ask how that works. Ideally, you want someone who can sell the book internationally and has some experience with film rights.

How long are you contracted with them and what's a reasonable amount of time to give them to sell your book? Typically, you'll be contracted for a year. A year should be enough time to sell a book, but then again you may spend that year editing with your agent.

There are many questions you could ask, but the above are the most important. I would Google search "questions to ask a prospective literary agent."

ALSO: NEVER PAY FOR AN AGENT; they only get paid when you sell books!

# 5
# Writing a Query Letter

When you submit to an agent or publisher, you will need to write a one-page query. Here are some guidelines to follow, as well as some sample query letters that landed me my first publishing contract and my first agent. I don't always follow these guidelines, but it's a good way to start.

First sentence: Give us a tagline for your book!

First paragraph: After the tagline, introduce the genre, the word count, and a couple of things about the story (tailored specifically to what the agent is looking for).

Second paragraph: Tell us about a character or two, and a bit more about the story, with a few sentences previewing the major conflict (think back-of-the-book blurb).

End with a couple of sentences about yourself, and again relate to the specific agent or publisher. Let them know you specifically researched them!

Use my queries as examples—the one about *Rabbit in Red* landed me an indie publisher and the one about *Darkness Calls* landed me my first literary agent.

And feel free to Google "Query Letter Tips." There's a lot of great advice online!

YOUR NAME
ADDRESS
E-MAIL
PHONE

Dear AGENT NAME SPELLED CORRECTLY,

Follow the rabbit, play the rabbit, save the rabbit, and then kill the rabbit. That's the mysterious Rabbit in Red challenge, a game created by eccentric film producer Jay Bell to recruit talented young minds for his horror empire. I envisioned an adventure as if Willy Wonka produced horror games and invited pop culture fanatics to battle in a great competition. I am seeking representation for my young adult thriller RABBIT IN RED, complete at 70,000 words. Throughout this adventure, you'll find young characters with heart, quirky characteristics, dark pasts, and great ambition.

Bill Wise, a high school senior, is a horror fan through and through, which is ironic considering he witnessed a home intruder murder his father a decade ago. He gets through the boring school days knowing he will get to rip on all the high school mediocrity with his best friend, Jaime Stein. Jaime lives across the country, and she sees a world of self-obsession around every corner. Bill and Jaime met online and initially bonded over losing loved ones at a young age. But it's not just life's big questions that bond the two. They share a passion for spine-tingling stories that keep them up late at night, and that mutual joy becomes an opportunity for escape and adventure.

Bill and Jaime learn of Jay Bell's challenge for young adults to earn an internship in the horror industry at his Rabbit in Red studio in California. But Jay doesn't care for applications or interviews. He wants to challenge horror enthusiasts through significantly more creative and elaborate methods.

First the contestants must solve a number of horror riddles to prove they are worthy. It's a pop culture enthusiast's dream, but that only provides the admission ticket. A series of exciting adventures await our group of young horror fanatics on location: 4D horror movie re-enactments where our contestants fight the killers, save the innocent, and even play the villain. But like the riddles, the simulations lead to much more. Throughout the challenges, some contestants go missing, and the purpose of Jay Bell's Rabbit in Red challenge becomes a mystery and the ultimate test of terror. The lines between fantasy and reality blur, as real threats endanger the lives of our characters.

I have published in various magazines. I'm a college professor and hope to become a lifelong novelist. My book is complete and stands alone, but I have many exciting ideas for a great series as well.

Thank you for your consideration. I will include the first chapter below, and I would love to send you the complete manuscript and work with you more soon.

Sincerely,
Joe Chianakas

Hi (INSERT AGENT'S NAME),

I am seeking representation for DARKNESS CALLS (YA fiction, 90,000 words). It is complete, unpublished, and is intended to be the first book of a new series. When browsing (INSERT AGENCY), you jumped off the page to me. It's not just because you seek YA, but also because you give me the impression that you take time to genuinely help your authors. I've worked very hard on my book, but I am always open to criticism and willing to improve. Let me tell you about my story.

The woods outside of Worthlapp High School lead to all sorts of evil and monsters, collectively called the Darkness. The Darkness feeds on children with great energies—webs of light that only it can see. The Darkness also guards a secret. Beyond the woods hides a powerful magic, the Fountain of Youth. Those magical waters enhance our webs of light.

The Darkness desires to consume these webs and transform itself into the Lark, the ultimate beast. It tried before, and although it took the lives of many, it failed to create the Lark. To assist it, it tasks teenagers Christina and Fiara to bring it new children.

Christina and Fiara fought the Darkness once before as kids, and although they survived, they certainly aren't the same. The Darkness destroyed Christina's family, and it turned Fiara into something not fully human. Now, it temporarily possesses Christina's body to gather the new kids it needs, like Lawson. Lawson has a uniquely yellow energy that represents a strong mentality, but he sure doesn't feel strong—he crushes on his best friend Teddy and struggles to come-out. Teddy doesn't notice Lawson's crush, though, because his mom is dying from cancer and doesn't have long to live.

But Christina isn't having it this time. She refuses to willingly kill for the Darkness, and she manages to break free from its hold on her. She gathers the ones it wanted dead and forms a small army instead. From all the turbulence of adolescence to life's biggest mysteries, a group of teenagers embark on a quest to save their friends and ultimately the world.

I am an enthusiastic and hard-working author and will work above and beyond for you if you represent me. My first book series, Rabbit in Red, was originally picked up by an indie publisher three years ago. When that publisher closed its doors, I decided to keep it as a self-published book. On my own, I negotiated deals with the biggest subscription boxes in the world. Those platforms purchased over 30,000 copies, and every single one of them came back to buy other books in the series, too, because of the great response from their customers. I've won indie awards, I consistently have one of the most downloaded books on Smashwords, and I have a string of media, music videos, short films, audiobooks, and more. In short, I've worked hard over the last few years and have successfully built a fandom anxiously awaiting Darkness Calls, and I want to take my work to the next level, by working with you. I am also a college professor.

Thank you for your consideration. I will include the first three chapters and a synopsis below.

Joe Chianakas
PHONE NUMBER
EMAIL

# 6
# The Writing Process

Okay, so we've previewed several steps and ideas for acquiring agents and publishers. Let's take a giant step back and talk about the writing process. This part, of course, is the most important part. Without a good manuscript, we shouldn't even be talking about publishing.

Here is my step-by-step writing process.

**STEP ONE: Write!** Set a goal to follow and write until your book is finished. I don't care if it takes a month or years.

My personal goal: I write 1000 words each day I'm writing. I write 3-5 days a week when I'm working on a new project. It's going to take me 15-20 weeks to finish a book at that pace, but it's a good goal for me. I've completed books within a month, which is possible, but also very stressful, especially if you have a fulltime job outside of writing. Why stress yourself out? Give yourself a reasonable goal.

Also, know when you write best. For me, it's first thing in the morning after breakfast and a cup of coffee. Sometimes I have to get up extra early before work. I put in an hour when my brain is fresh. I can do that a couple of times a week and then use the weekend. In a few months, I'll have a completed manuscript!

Again, tailor this to you. Maybe you need a 500 words per day goal. Maybe you need 2000 words per day but only write on the weekends. It doesn't matter. But learn what you need to do to be successful without causing too much self-stress. Stick to it, and you will have a finished book.

**STEP TWO: Celebrate!** Honestly, this is a big deal. Not everyone can finish a book. You need to take yourself out to dinner. Celebrate your success as we go, because the truth is that we have an awfully long way to go yet.

**STEP THREE: DETACH.** Put your manuscript away for a minimum of four weeks. Make yourself think about something else. I often go on a reading-binge during this time. Devour a few new books you've been meaning to read. The point is that you need some distance from your own work if you are going to able to honestly critique yourself.

**STEP FOUR: READ AND CRITIQUE.** It's time to go back through the manuscript and rip yourself apart. I like to print out a copy and make notes as I go. This is everything from structure, to plot, to character changes, to writing that needs to be improved. This could take a few weeks and be stressful. You need to be your biggest critic.

**STEP FIVE: REVISION #1.** Using your notes, go through the manuscript from the very beginning and rework the entire thing as needed.

(NOTE: You may want to repeat steps three through five as many times as needed until you feel comfortable moving forward. At a certain point, we need other people's help. You have to trust yourself to know when you need to ask for that.)

**STEP SIX: READING GROUP CRITIQUE.** Give your revised manuscript to an odd number (3, 5, or 7) of readers for feedback. (That way, if there's disagreement, consider the majority opinion.) Give them a month to read, then make a date for dinner.

You buy dinner (or make dinner) as a thank you for reading your book. Tell them you need honest feedback. Compliments are great, but they won't improve your book. This is not about typos or grammar—ask for feedback on everything related to the story, the writing, the characters, when they were bored, when they stopped reading, and more.

**STEP SEVEN: CRY.** Getting good feedback is hard. It's like listening to a group rip apart your child for an evening. Go cry, go exercise, go hit a punching bag—whatever you need to do. But remember, you are doing this to create the best book possible. You owe it to your art and to your future readers to give them the best product possible. So read, listen, and consider your group's feedback. Learn to accept criticism, but also remember it is your story and you can do whatever you want! Do NOT be defensive or make excuses. This may be a group, if you're lucky, that you can return to several times for help with future projects. Even if you disagree with them, value and respect their opinion and thank them for their time. Always end with a thank you. Sleep on the feedback for a couple days, and then proceed to the next step.

**STEP EIGHT: REVISE AGAIN**: Make the changes you want to make. Start at the very beginning, and revise based on the feedback of your reading group.

(NOTE: You may want to repeat steps six through eight again, perhaps with the same group or a different group. There's no limit on revising. The more you do this, the better your work will be.)

**STEP NINE: FIND AN EDITOR.** Ultimately, I recommend going through the book one more time with a professional editor, one person's opinion you respect. I've been fortunate to work with great editors I've found through my experiences, but I also have found incredible colleagues and friends with a natural talent for editing. This is the "final" edit (not if you do work with an agent or publisher, as you will repeat many of these steps again). But this is the final edit before querying or self-publishing. Find someone who enjoys going line by line and tightening your writing, looking for plot holes, and strengthening your characters. Edit and revise as you go. Some editors will do the entire book, and give it back to you. So, **REVISING AGAIN** is part of this step. Others like to do a few sections at a time, and you will revise as you work with them.

**STEP TEN: PROOFREAD.** I typically ask one person to help me proofread. This time, I do not want any feedback on the story. I just want to find nasty typos. After I get that back, I still run it through something like Grammarly. Keep in mind, it's rare to have a book be 100% perfect. Still, skipping this step is obvious to agents and publishers. Keep in mind, it doesn't matter how intelligent or educated you are. If you have revised a book several times, you become almost blind to your own errors. You really need someone's help here, so don't be shy. Ask for help.

**STEP ELEVEN: QUERY OR SELF-PUBLISH.** Now, you're ready. Decide what's the right path for you, and go for it!

NOTE: See how the actual writing is just a small part of this process! *Writing is about revising!*

# 7
# Revision Tips

I ended the last chapter with this note: See how the actual writing is just a small part of this process! *Writing is about revising!*

So, let me give you some revision tips that have helped me. I suggest that you find a writing partner, someone who is also working on a project, and do this activity together to help each other out. Additionally, these questions may assist you in developing a reading critique group. They may not know what to tell you or what to think about as they read, so consider giving them some of the questions below about style, characters, and plot.

PARTNER EXERCISE: VOICE

1. Read one page of your work aloud to a partner. Discuss: What sounded good? What sounded choppy? Initial reaction? This allows you to hear your own work, which can be beneficial in developing your writing voice.

2. Have your partner read one page (the next page if possible) of YOUR work aloud to you. Discuss again: what are the strengths and weaknesses you hear? Having someone else read your work can be terrifying but incredibly beneficial.

3. After both have done the above, then read silently BOTH pages you have written, plus one more. Mark up thoughts as you go. Don't worry about proofreading. We want to go deeper.

## THINGS TO LOOK FOR IN WRITING STYLE

1. Pay attention to sentence beginnings. Underline sentence beginnings that become repetitive (always starting with "the" or "he") and discuss how to vary that.

2. SHOW, DON'T TELL. Underline anything that tells us how a character feels or what a character does instead of showing us. Example: "Sue felt angry." Readers want to see it. Instead: "Sue clenched her fists and glared at James. Shaking her head, she opened her mouth and said . . ."

3. Advanced option: Take a page or two of your writing and label each sentence by sentence type: Simple (S), compound (C), complex (X), compound-complex (CX). Writers often fall into repetition—all simple sentences or only simple and compound. This takes time, so don't feel overwhelmed, but over time, you want to have a natural variety of sentence styles to enhance the flow of your writing.

## THINGS TO LOOK FOR IN CHARACTERS

1. Do your readers like them? Do your readers root for them? People like to read about characters they love and characters they hate. Ask your readers how they feel about your characters. Is that the reaction you wanted?

2. Ask your readers to describe your characters. Is that what you were going for? Everyone has an opinion here, but I side with Stephen King: give us some but not too many physical characteristics, and let the reader picture your characters. Writers

overdo this—describing every single thing a character is wearing to the lines in their faces. Avoid excessive details.

3. Ask your readers about your characters' dialogue. Does it sound believable? Does it sound how real people talk?

THINGS TO LOOK FOR IN PLOT

1.  Does anything not make sense? Any plot holes?

2.  Is it believable?

3. Do you want to keep reading? Does the conflict motivate the reader to want to know what is going to happen?

# 8
# A Reflection Exercise for Fiction

I've dug through my teaching files—things I've taken from many different sources throughout the years. Some of these exercises may have come from other classes, teachers, and workshops I've taken, so thank you to all who have helped me get to where I am.

These are some things that have helped me. Let's start by thinking about our favorite books.

What are some stories you really enjoyed? Chances are—those stories had magnificent plots. One event set into motion another event, each more captivating than the last.

PLOT brings everything together: the characters, the setting, the voice, and everything else into a single, organizing force.

What are some of the best stories you've enjoyed?
1.
2.
3.
4.
5.

THE QUESTION

Plot can often be summarized by a major, dramatic yes/no question. What are the yes/no questions you want answered in your story? Or—what are the yes/no questions that the readers should be considering?

With the top five stories you listed above, what is the major yes/no question with each story? List those below.
1.

2.

3.

4.

5.

YOUR STORY: What are your yes/no questions? List those below:

1.

2.

## CONNECTION TO CHARACTER

The biggest factor with characters is that they have DESIRE. So, let's examine our yes/no questions. Do they connect to your characters' desires? If not, how can we connect desire and plot to create those motivating questions?

## CONNECTION TO CONFLICT

Again, a character must desire something. Then, there must be obstacles to what he or she desires. Those obstacles create conflict, which drives our story forward. What are the obstacles your character faces?

## THE STRUCTURE OF PLOT

### THE BEGINNING
Drop the reader in the middle of the action.

Provide only the necessary background information to catch the reader up to speed.

Establish the major dramatic question.

THE MIDDLE

Obstacles, obstacles, obstacles!

Each obstacle/event is a part of a chain—a CONNECTED series of events.

Each obstacle should build in tension, be harder or worse than the previous.

THE END

What is the answer to the ultimate, dramatic question?

QUESTIONS FOR YOUR WORK:

What are the characters' desires? Do the desires connect with that central question?

What obstacles or challenges do the characters face? Do they intensify as the story progresses?

From what you read, what is believable? What isn't as believable?

What do you know about the characters' backgrounds based on what you read? Is it too much? Or not enough?

Are we dropped right into the action?

Are the obstacles connected?

What is (or what do you think, based on what you read) the answer to the ultimate dramatic question?

# 9
# A Reflection Exercise for Characters

## DESIRE

A character should want something and want something badly. What does your protagonist desire?

## HUMAN COMPLEXITY

What are the specific and unique details that make your character complex? Not a *type* of person but a *real* person.

What flaws does your protagonist have? Good characters are not perfect; good characters have flaws just like all of us.

## REFLECT ON YOUR STORY

1. What did the characters desire? Why do they want what they want?

2. What are some details that make your character seem real? What are some details that make your character more of a cliché or a type?

3. Do you like the character(s)? Why or why not?

4. Where in the writing is the author SHOWING us what the character thinks and does? Where in the writing is the author TELLING us instead?

5. Imagine: You are the editor. The publisher says you must cut 10% due to cost. What details or sections would you cut if you absolutely had to? (Now, authors—what can we learn from this?)

# 10
# Understanding your Story

Give us a one sentence description of your story, something you could tweet about, use in interviews, short/sweet, but makes us want more.

Now, give us a one to two paragraph back-of-the-book blurb. (Read examples from your favorite stories).

STORY BASICS

    A. How many main characters?

    B. Who is the "villain"?

    C. What is the conflict between the main character and the villain?

    D. Where does the story take place? Is this setting important?

E. Your job is to "make your character run up a tree (conflict), then have others throw stones at him/her (major conflict, make us feel!), then finally get them down (if you like happy endings)." Besides the main conflict, list other types of conflict that will appear in your story.

Man vs. Man:
Man vs. Nature:
Man vs. Himself:

F. Describe the ending you want to see. Happy, sad, tragic, etc?


IV. Outlining


Act I: The exposition and getting your main character up that tree. Describe the first third of the book.


Act II: He or she is up that tree. Now throw rocks! What happens in the middle of the story?


Act III: Outline the ending. What is the story's climax? Outline the resolution following the climax.


Option: Some writers outline every chapter. Some outline "acts." Some don't outline at all. You have to learn the best strategy that works for you.

# 11
# Finding Inspiration and Fresh Ideas

Where do you get your ideas? That's the biggest question writers receive, as if there is some magical place to go for story ideas. There's not. Ideas come and go. Some are good, and some are not. For me, the secret is in staying inspired and stimulated.

So, if you're looking for new ideas, I challenge you to not ask, "What can I write about?" But instead to ask, "What inspires and stimulates me?"

Focus on that. I'll share what works for me, and I hope it may help you. Like so much with this art, it's really about finding your own path.

## PODCASTS AND WALKING

I listen to podcasts every single day while walking (and I walk for miles every single day too). Now, I have a wonderful dog to help me stay active. I walk her multiple times a day (up to four miles a day), and when we walk, I listen to my favorite podcasts. I have found several to be inspiring. And yes, I've even gotten good writing ideas from some!

There's also something about exercise that stimulates creativity. Writing is so sedentary, obviously. If you are staring at a computer and trying to think of what to write (or get that infamous "writer's block"), then it's time to get outside and MOVE. There's science that backs this up—the mind develops better thoughts and ideas when one is moving compared to when one is sitting.

When I get ideas while walking, I take out my note app on my phone and jot them down. I have dozens of story ideas and points all documented in my note app. I return to those when I revise.

Now, we all have different tastes in entertainment, so I recommend you explore several podcasts to find what you enjoy, but I'll list a few to get you started.

For interviews: I love Armchair Expert with Dax Shepard and ID10T with Chris Hardwick. Both get deep with a variety of guest interviews (including authors!). Of course, not every interview is amazing, but I've gotten tons of inspiration from these two podcasts. They are a part of my weekly routine. You'll find artists in all areas of entertainment who are just as vulnerable and insecure as you may be. You'll hear advice and success stories. You'll listen to subjects that will surprise you and teach you something new (always a must for keeping our brains sharp and developing new characters).

For stories: My podcast gateway drug was *S-town* and the first season of *Serial*. Will you learn something that helps with your book or find life inspiration? Eh, maybe not. But they are excellent stories and they focus on deeply intriguing characters. And there's always something we can learn from that.

I have a dozen others I enjoy, but instead of listing those, start with the above. There are ones for writers too, but I think it's helpful to get outside of our worlds and heads now and then.


THE IMPORTANCE OF READING


Above all else, the biggest tip writers receive is that they must be readers. I cannot agree with this more. I've met self-published authors who have told me, "I wish I had time to read. I'm too busy writing." When I've looked at their books, I see dozens of errors, poor writing, and oh, guess what? No one is buying their books!

There is no better way to improve one's writing and one's voice than to read CONSISTENTLY all year long.

I look at it this way: Trying to be a writer without reading is like learning a foreign language by only speaking and refusing to listen to anyone use the language. How effective would that be?

It would be lousy.

Don't be that kind of writer. Yes, we have jobs, families, lives, and writing takes a lot of extra time. But if you don't make time for reading, then your writing will suffer.

When I'm struggling with something such as description (how can I describe characters without always saying the same thing?) or anything like that, then I turn to successful authors and read their work. I keep a sharp eye on how they use description and dialogue and everything else I'm trying to work on.

I also try to alternate the kinds of books I read. First, you must read within your genre. Become a literary expert with the books in your genre. But also explore other genres just to keep you on your toes. So, I often pick a young-adult book and alternate that with an adult novel of some kind.

Imitation is the greatest flattery, right? I'm not saying copy someone's ideas, but it's through reading that you will develop great ideas. For example, when I read a dystopian novel, I often get inspired with other ideas as to how our world could end up that way.

I have to balance my writing with my reading. As I discussed in the writing process chapter, I aim for 1000 words a day. When I'm super busy, I still schedule reading on those days, too. Maybe it's only twenty minutes or even just one chapter, but I make sure to read as often as I write.

Trust me on this—if you don't make time for reading, you will not be successful. Make time for it.

## GET OUTSIDE

Take hikes. Go on bike rides. Sit in nature with a notebook. For me, the ideas don't happen when I'm staring at a computer screen. My best ideas have hit me while I was outside doing some kind of activity or while reading a book.

## ASK PEOPLE WHAT THEY'RE READING

My favorite conversations are often about books. When you hear someone speak enthusiastically about a book and WHY they enjoyed it, that can also inspire and stimulate fresh ideas.

## GEEK OUT

Enjoy your favorite shows, music, video games, or whatever you like without guilt. There's a reason we love entertainment—it resonates with us intellectually and emotionally. I think about the stories that make me laugh, that make me cry, that I'd line up for at midnight to catch the latest release . . . I think about them and what I can learn from them when working on my own material.

So, the next time you find yourself asking, "What can I write about," consider changing the question. "Where can I find new inspiration and stimulation?"

That's what works for me, and I hope it will work for you.

Since I recommended podcasts, let me recommend a few of my favorite books that have inspired me recently. Any of these would be great if you're unsure what books you should pick up.

In incredibly written adult fiction that we can certainly learn something from: Kate Atkinson's *Case Histories*, Matthew

Sullivan's *Midnight at the Bright Ideas Bookstore*, Erin Morgenstern's *The Starless Sea*, Sarah Bailey's *The Dark Lake*, and Megan Miranda's *All the Missing Girls*. (*The Starless Sea* is truly a love letter to bibliophiles and one of the most poetically beautiful novels I've ever read—put that at the top of your list.)

In strong young-adult fiction: Karen McManus's *One of Us is Lying*, E. Lockhart's *We Were Liars*, Tamsyn Murray's *Instructions for a Second-hand Heart*, Neal Schusterman's *Unwind*, and Becky Albertalli's *Simon vs. The Homo Sapien's Agenda*.

# 12
# Redefining Success

There's a great story told in Mark Manson's *The Subtle Art of Not Giving a F\*\*\** about the lead singer in the metal band Megadeath. In short, apparently the lead singer in Megadeath used to be a part of the band Metallica but got kicked out. Frustrated and upset, he started his own band, which was hugely successful—millions of albums sold, thousands of sold-out concerts. But in an interview, the lead singer described himself as a failure "because his band never was a big as Metallica."

It's a great story, and I recommend Manson's book if you struggle with esteem issues (as we all do). It puts many things in perspective.

The truth is that all artists will struggle with self-worth and self-esteem. What if no one buys my book? What if no one likes my book?

I remember feeling so incredibly nervous at my first book signing. The same questions flooded my mind. What if no one shows up?

There will be a question at every step of this process. I am convinced we have to redefine our expectations and perceptions of success.

If you wrote a book, that is success! Not many can do that. I don't care if you do not sell a single copy. You deserve to celebrate your accomplishment!

To me, writing a book and becoming a local author is like being the star of a play at the community theater. Sure, perhaps that performer would love to star in a Broadway show or a hit movie. Maybe he or she has dreams of acting full-time and even being a name recognized around the world.

Deep inside, we know that such success will only happen to a few lucky and talented souls. It's easy to be jealous (and it's human to be jealous), but we have to look at our own lives, not the lives of others.

Here is what I would say to that community theater star: you are in a great production! You may have dozens or even hundreds of people watching you on a Saturday night, cheering for you at the end of your show.

*That is success!*

I am constantly torn between where I am now and where I want to be, just like all of you, I imagine. In the writing world, we want to have a book be written, we want it to get published, we want it to be a bestseller, we would love to make a fulltime income just from writing, to be well-reviewed, to get movie deals, to become a name everyone knows . . .

Take a deep breath. I work at this one-step at a time by first recognizing and celebrating the success I have and then by creating an ambitious and realistic goal as to what I want to do next.

If you self-publish a book, that is success! If you have someone buy your book, that is success. If someone compliments your book, that is success.

Do you need thousands of sales and compliments? (Sure, you want them, but do you *need* them?)

I can't imagine what it would be like to have as many sales and concerts as the band Megadeath has had and still view myself as a failure. Let's not go down a similar path of self-criticism.

Still, I understand that most of you will want more than a single sale or one good review. Having goals drives us forward and keeps us working. Goals are good, but we have to reflect on our esteem issues.

I wrote a book and celebrated that success, then I made a goal to get it published.

After a lot of rejection and hard work, I got it published and celebrated that. A few people bought it. I wanted more to buy it. I created goals to make that happen, but I celebrated every sale and every review along the way.

At the end of the day, we can't compare ourselves to others. You may find yourself at a book event one day where one author is selling ten books to your one. You will find yourself online and see that you have one review, and someone else has one-hundred. In the age of social media, it's too easy to compare and despair.

You may never be Stephen King or J.K. Rowling.

No, scratch that. You will never be them. That's the truth.

Instead, you will be uniquely YOU. And guess what? Your readers who discover your books are very unlikely to have had a conversation with King or Rowling. They are unlikely to know anything about them on a personal level that they haven't read in a book or learned in an interview.

Your readers—your friends, family, coworkers, neighbors, community members—will know you.

And that, my friends, is success.

# 13
# Self-Publishing Formatting and E-Books

If you have decided to self-publish, congratulations! You are about to become a published author. There are many pros to self-publishing. You are in full control of your work. You will not share royalties with anyone else. You get to decide when and how often you publish.

Do not let anyone say you are less of an author for choosing this route. The truth about many of the other options is that it's often about luck. Editors and agents—like you and me—have moods. Who knows what kind of mood they are in when they read our pitch? Self-published authors have gone on to find just as much success as authors with agents. It can be done.

The reality is, though, that it's up to you to do all the work.

My job is to help you. So, let's take a look at self-publishing step-by-step.

We will explore formatting, ebook publishing, and print-on-demand.

## FORMATTING TIPS

This will allow you to self-publish or have your manuscripts already polished for publishers and agents (they like that!). If you have a finished manuscript, go back through it and set up this formatting.

1. Never use "tab" to indent. Instead, go to the paragraph word icon (see below), then click "line spacing options," then in the indentation section click "special," then "first line," then "0.5." This

will make you auto indent whenever you press enter. You'll need to repeat this step if you change alignment.

2. At the end of each section or chapter, insert a page break. Even for title pages, copyright pages, dedication pages, etc.

3. Keep font simple. Times New Roman 12 dor all text.

4. You can center chapter headings (chapter one) to Times New Roman 14 bold.

## AMAZON E-BOOK SELF-PUBLISHING

1. Set up an account at kdp.amazon.com.

2. Have your manuscript saved in Microsoft Word or a similar program (you can upload .doc, .docx, mobi, epub, or HTML). Kindle does not want a PDF because they want readers to be able to change font settings to their preference.

Formatting reminders:

A. Avoid special fonts and colors.
B. Chapter headings can be bold and centered, but text font should be simple: Times New Roman.

C. NO TABS.

D. Insert page breaks at the end of each chapter. Also check to see if you inserted page numbers and headers for your name/book title

E. If you have images, insert them only as JPEG and make sure they are aligned in the center.

Other Setup Reminders:

A. You generally have a title page with your book title and name. Then insert page break.

B. Have a copyright page. Can be as simple as:

C. Have a dedication page (third page). "For . . ."

D. Then your entire book.

E. I often like to end with an additional acknowledgment section or author's note, thanking everyone who helped me write, edit, and publish.

3. Have a back-of-the-book teaser ready to go (this goes under "description"), as well as the genres in which you want to list your book. Amazon lets you choose two. Choose the two most appropriate (for example, I do horror and mystery, or horror and thriller).

4. Add contributors. You will add your name for author, but have the option to list others, if you want to list a cover designer or editor.

5. There are other options—like age range and grade range. I leave these blank.

6. Upload your cover. (If you don't have one, I'll explore some options for you below.)

7. Upload your book, and you're ready to go!

The publishing process generally takes at least 12 hours before you will see the book live.

OTHER THINGS TO CONSIDER ON AMAZON:

_____ 1. Price? I like the idea of a release sale of just 99 cents. If you can spread the word well, this will help you get a good rank on Amazon, which may get you noticed by others! You will choose 35% royalty rate on a 99 cent sale.

_____ 2. Later: make it whatever you want. Depending on how well my books do, the ebooks go from $1.99-$3.99. Once you make the price the higher, you can collect 70% royalty. Note: it may take 90 days before you will get any royalty checks.

_____ 3. KINDLE UNLIMITED? This is a cool feature. If you choose to make your book available on Kindle Unlimited (like Netflix for books), you cannot upload your ebook anywhere else. That means no Nook, no iTunes, etc. BUT for new authors, I think Kindle Unlimited is the way to go. You can always remove your book later and upload ebook elsewhere. Plus, ebook readers don't need a Kindle to read. Amazon has a free Kindle app that you can download on any smart phone, tablet, or computer. With KU, you get paid per page read if a subscriber chooses your book.

_____ 4. Create an Amazon author page and bio: https://authorcentral.amazon.com/ This will allow you to post an author bio, gain Amazon followers, and see author ranking.

_____ 5. Ask family and friends to post reviews for you. This really helps! But don't post more than one review from one household (Amazon will delete all reviews! They check for spam/cheating with reviews—more on this in chapter eighteen.)

SPECIAL NOTE ON CHILDREN'S BOOKS:

Amazon has specific templates you will need to follow, if you are publishing picture books. You will need to go to this site: https://kdp.amazon.com/en_US/how-to-publish-childrens-books
Then download the specific template for children's books.

**Options besides Amazon:**

Go to Smashwords.com! You'll upload to Smashwords very similarly. Smashwords distributes ebooks through Nook, iTunes, Kobu, and more. If you do NOT make your book available for Kindle Unlimited, you can upload your e-book to BOTH Amazon and Smashwords.

General advice for first time e-book self-publishing:

Start with Amazon and do Kindle Unlimited for six months. If it's still selling, stick with Kindle Unlimited. If it's not selling, remove it from the unlimited program and add to Smashwords, too.

Sales are all about marketing and promoting. There's a big chapter on that in this book, too!

## COVER OPTIONS

Amazon has a cover designer you can use for your ebook. It's pretty generic, but it also doesn't cost anything. You can play with those cover options when you upload your ebook.

However, you may want to hire a cover artist or graphic designer for your book. One of the least expensive options is to purchase a pre-made cover, to which you fill in your title and author information. One site at the time of this writing that offers pre-made covers at very reasonable rates (under $100) is https://bookcoverzone.com/

The site claims that once a cover is sold, no one else can purchase it either—so the cover is unique to your book.

Of course, a great option is to hire someone to create an original design for you. This way you get what you want, and you can pitch a concept to the artist, if you have a cover in mind. If you don't have these resources, though, BookCoverZone is a great place to start!

If you hire an artist, there are a few things you should check:

1.  See his or her portfolio to know the kind of work they do, and make sure that seems like a good fit for your book.
2.  Pitch your idea, and be open to interpretations. A good artist can make your vision come to life.
3.  Make sure the text is easy to read (title and author).
4.  Be cautious of revisions. Most will let you revise a few times, but you may want to ask about revisions up front—how many can you get for the cost you've set?
5.  What files will you get upon completion? You want at least a .pdf and .jpg file as well as the front, the back, and

the entire layout in separate files so that you can use these for promotional purposes.

How much will hiring a cover artist cost you? It depends. Some have flat rates. Some will quote you after you tell them what you want (depending on the complexity of the design). Are you having something hand-drawn or is this graphic design? These are all things to consider.

For my *Rabbit in Red* series, I used cover artist Camron Johnson. You can view his work at http://www.camronjohnson.com/ and inquire about original design there.

You can also Google search for artists. There is no shortage of artists for hire on the web who do this kind of work: Google "book cover artists." If you go to events where artists display work, you can always collect information and ask them in person if they do cover art.

As for cost: I would expect to pay at least $200. I would be very hesitant to pay any more than $350.

For the cover of this book: I used a picture that was professionally edited, an author picture someone took of me a few years ago. Then I used Amazon's cover creator. Considering I had already purchased the photo and that Amazon's cover creator is free to use: the cover of this book did not cost me anything to do. Free is always a nice option, but the cover creator program is very limited in what it can do (best to have your own picture to use, if you choose that option).

# 14
## Self-Publishing for Print Books

Self-publishing for ebooks is fun and relatively easy, especially with Kindle. Ebooks are books, and you don't need to have print, if you don't want print.

If you're similar to me, though, the real joy in reading and writing comes from having a print book in hand. Nothing beats it.

And the best news for self-published authors is that you can have the same kind of quality print book as a *NY Times* bestselling author. And it won't cost much (or anything) to make it happen!

Let's walk through the steps you need to get your manuscript ready for print.

MARGINS AND PAPER SIZE

For print books, you'll need special margins.

The following would be for a 6 X 9 print book. There are many size options, and this may vary, especially for children's books, so always do your research. As a default, you can use a 6 X 9 size, which is the size of this very book that you are using. Here's how to set up your manuscript for a standard 6 x 9.

In WORD, go to "Page Layout." Then select "Size." Then "More Paper Sizes." You will then select "Custom Size" and make the width 6 inches and the length 9 inches.

Then, you will need to change margins. You will insert custom margins. Margins must be MIRRORED and labeled the following for 6 x 9.

Top: 0.94, Bottom: 0.94, Inside 0.9, Outside: 0.6

That's it. You're almost ready to print!

# PUBLISHING PRINT BOOKS

## OPTIONS FOR SELF-PUBLISHING PRINT BOOKS

Note: There are dozens of companies and "publishers" that will help you self-publish your book. The truth is that all they are doing is publishing your book through Amazon or Ingram, the two options I am explaining below. They do not have a different print option. They are just doing the work for you, charging you for it, and/or taking a cut of your royalties.

You can do all of this on your own!

Then you don't pay anyone to do it, you maintain complete control, you order what you want/when you want at the lowest wholesale cost, and you don't share royalties with anyone else.

Unless the following information completely overwhelms you, then I would avoid ever paying anyone to do this for you, and that includes royalties.

Let's remember what a real publisher should be doing for you: They provide you with an editor and cover art, which you do not pay for. They format and proofread, which you do not pay for. They help market your book by contacting reviewers and promoting it consistently on social media, which you do not pay for. Your publisher is successful if you sell books because they are taking a percentage of royalties for each sale. That's it.

Other so-called "publishers" often manipulate new authors into thinking that they will do everything I mentioned in the last paragraph. Instead, all they do is upload your book for you on either Amazon or Ingram, which you can do on your own.

How do you tell the difference between an authentic publisher and what we call a vanity publisher (a fake publisher, really)? It comes down to the querying and editing process. It should not be easy to get one—you query, submit a sample, they request the full if interested. From there, you should be working with an editor at no cost. Vanity publishers often make deals right away and there is no mention of editing (or, if there is, they will charge you for it).

Review the information in the chapters on indie publishing. Research any and all publishers who offer you deal, and be sure to talk with actual authors they've published. Ask the authors if they had to pay. Ask about the editing process. If they had to pay anything or if there was no real editing, then run away as fast as you can from that offer.

Okay, that's my big disclaimer, as I just don't want anyone to get manipulated. Let's get to work and discuss the difference between Amazon and Ingram for print self-publishing.

**If this is your first time ever self-publishing to print, you can do everything on Amazon—it's cheaper and easier when it comes to the technology you need.**

If you want books to be available for purchase outside of Amazon and you are willing to spend a little money for ISBNs and may have access to computer programs such as Adobe Acrobat, then Ingram (I argue) has more advantages.

But it's up to you!

AMAZON KDP FOR PRINT

You can get a paperback print-on-demand available on Amazon relatively easily.

The pro for Amazon: It's free, unlike Ingram, which often (but not always—there are free months!) charges a setup fee. You also get a free ISBN to use with Amazon.

The cons—your book is available to purchase on Amazon, but can be very limited to buy anywhere else. Also, Amazon does not accept returns. To get your books in major outlets, books typically must be returnable if they do not sell. Still, if this is your first time, Amazon is the easiest way to self-publish. That's how this very book was printed and published.

### INGRAM FOR PRINT

With Ingram, you can get your book pretty much any way you want it, including hardcover. I wouldn't choose hardcover, as it's really expensive.

The pros for Ingram: It has a bigger distribution system. Your book will be available not only in Amazon (yes, it's still available there!) but also online at major retailers like Barnes & Noble and Wal-Mart. Keep in mind these stores will not purchase your book to put on shelves, but people can buy it online from them. To get inside major stores requires reader demand. Readers can go inside any Wal-Mart or Barnes & Noble and request a copy of your book.

More pros: Your books are available at bigger discounts for retailers. You can also choose to make them returnable. Although you eat the cost of returned books, this is the main way to get your books in stores like Barnes & Noble. Keep in mind, just having a book on Ingram isn't going to automatically get your book in those stores. Readers have to request it. So again, Amazon's publishing program is likely to be easier for you.

The cons: It sometimes costs to upload your book. But if you check their site and follow their newsletters and social media, you'll find several promotions throughout the year to do free uploads. Usually, Ingram runs a free promotion after November each year. You also need to purchase an ISBN, which could cost you up to $125.00. An ISBN is the standard system used to identify books numerically. Every print book must have an ISBN. Ebooks do not need one.

So, it may be more difficult to first upload an ebook to Amazon and then upload a print book to Ingram. If this is your first time, you may want to make it easier on yourself and do it all through Amazon. That's fine. Learn and see how that goes! You can always remove a book from Amazon and upload it later to Ingram. It's totally up to you!

UPLOADING TO AMAZON

First, Amazon does make you set up bank account info and tax info so that you get paid (and so, of course, that you claim it on your taxes). Make sure you have that information ready before you publish.

Once your ebook is on Amazon, getting it available via print is very easy.

1. Click "CREATE PAPERBACK" at the bottom of your ebook title.
2. Just as you did for ebook, go through and double check that you have all settings correct, such as categories.
3. For ISBNs, click the free ISBN option. Note: If you decide to use Ingram at a later time, you will need a different ISBN.
4. When it comes to printing, the standard will be selected for you. Standard is cream paper with matte cover for fiction (or glossy cover and white paper for non-fiction), but change it if you want to do so.
5. Upload your carefully double checked manuscript as a PDF.
6. Upload your print cover as a PDF or create your own with Amazon's cover creator.

(Note: Amazon has a template you can download for covers. You need the full wrap on this; meaning—you need the front and the back cover uploaded to this section. Amazon will add its own bar code, if you don't already have one. You need to select the appropriate trim size, such as 6x9, and enter the correct number of pages so that the spine is of appropriate thickness. You also must have a minimum of 24 pages in the book to get a paperback. You can always add blank pages as needed. Also note—this book at just over one-hundred pages did not have a thick enough spine for Amazon to print the title on the spine.)

7. Preview the book.
8. Set your price (it all depends on length—set it so you make at least a few bucks off each book).
9. Launch it! (*Tip: Get a proof copy mailed to you first and double-check everything before making it available publicly.*)

Congratulations! Your print-on-demand book is now available for you and others to purchase (or it will be within 24-48 hours).

UPLOADING TO INGRAM

Set up an account at https://myaccount.ingramspark.com/

What you need:

_____ Your 6 x 9 formatted manuscript (or other size) saved as a PDF.

_____ Your full cover wrap, including front, spine, and back sized correctly and saved as a PDF.

_____ You will need an ISBN to sell print books. ISBNS are expensive. To purchase an ISBN, go to https://www.myidentifiers.com/. A single ISBN is about $125. You can buy a pack of ten ISBNS for $295. Your best bet is to work with a group and have everyone pitch in for ten. Then each ISBN would only cost you $30 or so. Contact your fellow local authors and/or start networking with others. This is how you save money. I would buy the ten pack, because ISBNs do not expire. You have ten now for life, and you can sell these to other authors too.

_____ Pricing: I recommend between $9.99 and $14.99, but you'll be able to play around with this. It really depends on the length of the book and cost of print for you. You want to make a couple bucks off each copy, but you don't want to make it so high that no one will buy it.

_____ Set up for paper type and cover: For fiction books, the standard is off-white for paper with a matte cover. Choose white paper and glossy cover for non-fiction. Of course, you can do whatever you want here.

COVER

Ingram has a template they will create and send to you and/or your cover designer. Use this form: https://myaccount.ingramspark.com/Portal/Tools/CoverTemplateGenerator

You will need your ISBN when you do this and the retail cost of your book. When you use the cover template above, Ingram will give you links to calculate cost. You will put in the size of your book (such as 6 X 9) and the page numbers. It will tell you how much your wholesale cost will be. Add to that whatever you want to make on the book. So, if my wholesale cost is $7 and I want to make at least $5 per copy, then I will retail the book at $12.00. You're in control—set the cost at whatever you want!

PDF/X

I also purchased Adobe Acrobat to save the best PDF files. Ingram likes files saved as PDF/X, which is easy to do on Adobe. Word can only convert to PDF. The difference is just with printing quality.

Okay, so Ingram may sound like a lot, but I promise you that once you walk through it a few times, it becomes pretty easy.

If this does sound like a lot, then stick with Amazon KDP for both print and ebook for your first time. It's easier to upload. Regular PDF is fine, so you only need Microsoft Word. You don't need to buy ISBNs or pay an uploading fee.

Both Amazon and Ingram offer support help. If you have questions while you are uploading, you can contact them and they will be able to help you.

*TIP: Be patient with all of the above. Do one step at a time. I know it can seem overwhelming just reading this. I promise you can do this, and if you take it just one step at a time, you will get there!*

# 15
# Amazon Author Profile

Once your book is live on Amazon, you will want to login to a separate system from Amazon KDP. It's Amazon Author Central—go here: https://authorcentral.amazon.com/

The first thing I would do is click the "books" tab and then "add more books." Search for your book, and sync it here to Author Central.

Then click on "Author Page." Here's where you add a short biography that will be included on your Amazon page. If you have a blog (which we will discuss in marketing), you can also add a link to that here. Upload an author photo as well, and a link to your website if you have one.

Although I wouldn't obsess over these, you can also check your sales ranks and customer reviews here.

Lastly, there is a "help" tab. If you have any questions about your book on Amazon, I've found the customer service here to be pretty good. There's a list of help topics you can explore to learn more about having your book on Amazon, such as editing editorial reviews.

# 16
# Building Local Community Support

## BOOKSTORES

I am lucky to live in perhaps one of the most supportive communities ever when it comes to local authors. I hope that you have a similar support system wherever you live, but if not, then you might just be the person to get the ball rolling for local author support.

To start, I would visit every local bookstore you have. Know the owner's name. Shop there! You don't want to show up with books one day and hope they will buy some. Be a regular shopper who they already know, which will make supporting you even easier.

When you do have a published book, then politely ask if they would be willing to stock them. Having your book on the shelf gives you some exposure, and you can tell readers to go buy your books at those stores, creating a mutually beneficial relationship.

Prior to your release, I would contact one or two local bookstores to see if you can do a book signing, too. The biggest lesson I learned early on is that you have to take some risks and ask these questions yourself. With few exceptions, no one is likely to be knocking on your door begging you to come do an event. You have to go out and find/create the events.

Be sure you support your local bookstores on social media as well. Like and share their pages, and they will likely do the same for you!

Maintain a relationship with these businesses by visiting when you can, liking/sharing/commenting on their social media posts, and always be grateful for their support. No one owes you anything. A sour attitude, cockiness, a lack of appreciation—those are ways to make sure you never see your book in someone's store.

## RELATED BUSINESSES

What are some other independent businesses that may be willing to sell your book? Think of places that have something in common with your genre. I visited some comic book stores and asked if they would be willing to display and sell a few books. I would plan on a 70-30 split for most stores, by the way. That means whatever the retail cost of your book is, you would get 70% of that for each sale, and the store would get 30%. That's pretty standard, but some may even give you 75 or 80%. I doubt anyone is getting rich off these sales, so don't argue this point. Again, be grateful and appreciative for those willing to give it a home!

What other kinds of businesses in your community might be willing to support? You don't know if you don't ask. Maybe an antique store or a bakery. Think of all the specialty stores you have. If your book involves cooking, maybe there are some local cafes that would display it. Find those unique connections. Maybe you have a children's book about nature, so you talk to your local park district or orchard to see if they would take some.

Also, many businesses may be more comfortable taking books if they do not have to pay you until after they sell. Be flexible with how you arrange that.

The point here is to get your book displayed in as many places as possible. Maybe someone won't buy it the first time they see it, but if they keep seeing it—that's good advertising, and that will help your book get known, at least locally.

## LOCAL EVENTS

We haven't discussed how much money you can make selling books, and the reason for that is twofold. One—it's not going to be the same for everyone. And two—it's unlikely to be anything worth bragging about.

I've been doing this long enough that yes, I have had months where I made more from book sales than I did in my full-time job. But that is rare and hard to do. I've also had months where I made maybe three bucks in royalties.

Getting a book published does not mean it will sell. If you are in this for money, you are in this for the wrong reason, and you will likely be very disappointed.

However, we do want to make some money. We put a lot of time into our work. Locally, the best way to make a profit is by selling books at events and festivals. Find those, go to those, watch and learn. Network with those authors. What promotional material do they use? How do they pitch their book? How did they get involved in the festival? Ask those questions!

Think of the seasonal events you have in your community—summer and fall festivals and other special events. If there's an event with someone at a table selling something, that's the kind of event you want to consider. Ask yourself, of course, if that's your audience. Are the people visiting those events likely to buy your book? I wouldn't sign up for every event, but if you think you might be able to sell a few, then this is a great way to promote your work. I've had one-day or weekend events like this where I've made several hundred dollars. That's nice. Of course, I've had events where I didn't sell a single copy either. You have to be prepared for that, too. It can be especially hard if you're working all week and then spend all weekend traveling or working at an event. So, choose wisely, but get yourself out there.

In addition, consider what you can sell to help promote your book or just to attract people to visit your booth. I've seen people sell charms, soaps, candles, T-shirts, pillows. I've seen people give bookmarks, recipes, magnets . . . find something to tie into your book release and you may attract more people this way, too.

## LIBRARIES AND BOOK CLUBS

Like bookstores, get yourself in your local libraries, too. Here, it's more than getting your book on a shelf. Your libraries are centers of activity within your community. They put on events all the time. Find an event to be a part of, or pitch an event idea. You might propose your book as part of a book club, where you attend as a guest speaker. Or you might do a reading or talk about writing and publishing or about the subject matter of your book. I often do talks on horror, and I know many author friends who do talks on ghosts (because they write ghost stories) or southern cooking (because they feature that in their story). Become an expert on a subject related to your book, and propose these ideas to your local libraries.

Book clubs aren't just at libraries. Search your community and schools for book clubs of all ages. If you think your book would be an appropriate fit, contact the club and pitch an idea to do a book club featuring a local author!

## SCHOOLS

Elementary schools, high schools, and colleges are another great resource. First, know your audience. If you are writing a children's book, you probably aren't contacting high schools to do a visit. But you are certainly contacting those grade school teachers and letting them know you'd love to visit and do a reading! (And maybe you can bring a couple copies for the school's library to buy?) You also could contact your local college's creative writing classes. Maybe you could share with them how you wrote that children's book!

I think about the subject matter and the themes of my book. Some of my books are in the horror genre, but they also have themes of bullying. So, why not contact a high school English class and say that I would visit to talk about those themes and more? In these situations, I wouldn't ask for a payment to come speak. Early in your career, you may need to build that audience first before you ask for too much. But you could get creative and say something like, "While I do not charge a speaking fee, I always ask—if possible—for the school to purchase ten books to give away to the class in random drawings."

I've done that before, and it generates excitement with the audience to know they can win something. And you sell at least ten books or however many you propose.

Tip: Suggest this to your local libraries, too! They have a book-buying budget, after all.

A FINAL THOUGHT

In general, I try to keep an open mind to what's happening in my community. I read the newspaper and keep up on local events. Would my book pair well with a movie release? A museum exhibit? A Halloween event? Why not just keep an open mind and be willing to ask big questions when it comes to what's happening in your community?

You will find unique ways of pairing up your book with various businesses and events if you train your mind to think this way.

(I once had a group fitness class give away copies of my horror novel. What was that connection? Well, the fitness class was doing a Halloween party!)

Lastly, it's about support. You get the support you give. Remember that, and you just may find a thriving community ready to do anything they can to help promote your work.

# 17
# Marketing

This is the longest chapter in the book because once you have a book out there that you want to sell, it's up to you to sell it. I don't care if you are self-published or working with big publishers. We're going to have to do a lot of work if we want to sell our books.

With social media at its peak, there are a number of great ways for authors to promote their work, but it can be overwhelming, too. Keep in mind this is something you will need to do whether you have an agent, publisher, or are self-published.

In fact, one agent (not mine) once actually told me, "I don't know why you'd want an agent or publisher, if you sell well on your own. All the work for promoting the book is still in your hands. No one has an advertising budget."

The truth is that good publishers are using the same tips I'm going to tell you, and it takes a team of people doing this to make it work. Even if you're self-published, you'll want to find a team to help you. We'll talk about that.

Let's explore several different areas you can use.

FACEBOOK

With Facebook, you can create an author page and a personal account of course. I would use both when trying to build excitement for your book release, and I would use an author page to try and consistently build an audience.

On your personal page, post about your writing and your book however you want. But let's take a note of caution—be careful about over-posting. I've seen author friends post about their work multiple times a day, trying to get people to buy it. And I'm not talking about just one day—some people spend weeks or months behaving like this. That's a good way to get unfollowed. People will stop caring.

Be honest and vulnerable. Create a plan leading up to your release.

A month or so before, post something like: "Friends, so I finally did it—my book is coming out on ____. I am hoping you will support me. When it gets closer, I am going to drop some links and events and I hope you'll forgive my excitement, but I really need your help to make it a success!"

Share your cover art. Create a cover page on Facebook using your cover art and a release date.

If you do pre-orders, promote those too of course.

When the book releases, go crazy for a couple days.

"It's here on sale for only ____! I would love your support, friends. Please get a copy and share with your friends!" (Be sure to include the link in your post.)

So, do that on your personal Facebook page and come up with a variety of ways to ask for help. Then, calm down a bit. You will annoy your friends if all you do is post about your book.

It's time to focus on your author page instead.

## FACEBOOK AUTHOR PAGE

Create a page that people can like and follow. This should be the exact name you use on your cover, so if you go by a pen name or initials, create the page in the same fashion.

During a book release, promote your book on your page the same way I described above for your personal profile on Facebook. With a page, you have a chance now to reach fans and to advertise.

First, you need to get some likes on it, so invite your friends to like the page. You can send an invite link and post about it your personal profile. I would only create one page. It allows you to focus your energy on one account. Plus, if you plan on inviting friends to like it, trust me that they may not want to see twelve different pages you've created on their newsfeed.

Next, for a book release, it's all about advertising. This is when you need to drop a few bucks into Facebook ads. Advertising is the number one way to sell books.

Hopefully, you do have friends and family who support your release, but what happens when all of them have bought a copy? You have to build an audience elsewhere.

So, once you have a page, you can advertise, and it's very easy to set up.

After you have created an author page, go to https://www.facebook.com/adsmanager

Click the green "create" ad button.

There are several options to choose from next, but I generally pick "engagement." Engagement helps Facebook send your ad to those it determines are most likely to interact with it.

Create a campaign name so you can keep track of it, such as "Book release ad one." Then click "continue."

Now, you get to customize your audience. First, you can narrow your age range, IF you think it's best for your book. Even though I write young adult, I generally keep the 18-65 age range as is. But if you think your audience is older, than maybe narrow it down a little, but not too much.

You can also choose your location. I keep mine set for all of the United States, but when I do local events, I come back here and select the city in which my event takes place. Or sometimes I focus on other countries and promote to Canada or the UK.

Detailed targeting is where it gets really fun. I want to narrow my audience to make sure the ones who see it are likely to buy it.

Here's an example I do for horror:

In the above example, I selected first people who had interest in Stephen King, *Stranger Things*, *Supernatural*, and *The Walking Dead*. I figured that gives me a good base of horror fans. But I want to narrow and tighten my audience, so I selected NARROW

FURTHER and kept adding demographics. I added must also match reading. Then must also match Halloween or horror movies. And so on. By selecting "AND MUST ALSO MATCH" that means I am getting an audience who first must like either Stephen King, *Stranger Things, Supernatural,* or *The Walking Dead* AND ALSO must like reading AND ALSO must like Halloween . . .

Notice my audience is still pretty broad, according to Facebook. So I would play with that until I get a defined audience, or until I feel I've exhausted possibilities.

Facebook is constantly changing advertising, but it is actually fun to play with.

From there, you want to add your link and a good, concise post that describes your link.

Example: "If you love a good murder mystery, try INSERT TITLE, on sale for only INSERT COST."

Once you get reviews, you can add some quotes and other things to keep mixing it up.

Also, pay attention to the ads you see on Facebook that catch your attention. I also look at images and short taglines that really pop, and I try to mimic those to create my own powerful ads.

You will need to create a budget on Facebook, too. This depends on what you're willing to spend. I usually do five dollars a day for one week. If the ad works and I'm selling books, I may extend it. If it's not working, I create a new ad, again playing with the wording of my post, any images I share, and tailoring demographics.

Once you start spending money on Facebook, you may get an email from them to review your marketing. It's a free phone call, and I highly recommend it. You will have someone chat with you on the phone while helping you customize your ad. I've learned a lot in just a couple phone calls, so don't ignore that email when it comes. I have noticed that you may need to spend a couple hundred bucks before they give you that call, though.

So, after some time, you hopefully will build a real fan base on your author page, maybe a couple hundred, maybe even a few thousand. That would be great.

Like your personal profile, I would not constantly post about your own book every day (or even every week). Use your page to create a real fandom of like-minded readers. I post about the books and movies I'm watching. I geek out on my page. I post motivational quotes and little stories that I think my readers would enjoy about my life. And sure, a couple times a month, I will still post a good review for one of my books or something about my books to keep them alive. But those who only post about their own work will surely be seen as only self-serving if not really annoying.

Also, you can schedule posts on your Facebook page. So, if you have a busy week, you can always take a Sunday to create a few funny or motivational posts and have them scheduled throughout the week to post automatically. This saves you some time, but also keeps your page active.

FACEBOOK GROUPS

Another trend I've seen on Facebook are the group pages. Some people create book clubs related to their genres. I would start by focusing on your page. Then I would search for groups to join. Find ones that you value and ones that you would enjoy contributing to. Maybe you'll find a good book club page, and they'd be willing to share your new release when the time comes. Or you'll get ideas about what kind of group to create. But keep in mind that you may need to build your audience before creating several different things on Facebook. When you've been published for a year and you're working on your second book, come back to this idea. Google "creative ways to promote books on Facebook." You'll get plenty of fresh ideas.

## INSTAGRAM AND TWITTER

Before you advertise on Facebook, create an Instagram profile, too. Instagram, as you probably know, is focused on images. You can also link it to your author page on Facebook, so that when you do one ad on Facebook, it will actually promote both on Facebook and Instagram, giving you a larger audience.

The best part about Instagram for promoting work is the use of hashtags. Just like Facebook, when you have a release coming out, be sure to also share it on Instagram and use good hashtags. I generally use the following:

#bookstagram          #instabook          #currentlyreading
#authorsofinstragram          #writersofig          #bookclub
#bookrecommendation          #mustread

There are dozens more. Browse any of the above hashtags on Instagram and make notes as to the other tags that are being used on those posts.

Caution: Don't use Instagram to *only* promote your work or once again you will be that super annoying social media person who appears totally self-serving. Use Insta to geek out on what you love. I take a picture of every book I read and post it with a short review, using the tags I've described above. I post pictures of my animals or nature and dozens of other things because I want to be authentic and genuine and NOT totally self-serving.

With Instagram and Twitter, there's a big follow-for-follow community.

Personally, I dislike it. I admit that when I first received my publishing contract, I went on Twitter and spent a good month in the follow-for-follow game. It goes like this: especially with writers, the rule of thumb is that if a writer follows you, you should follow them back. That's mutually supportive. The problem I have isn't the support. The problem I have is that the social media platforms become overwhelming if I am following thousands of others. It's too much.

So, maybe I'm the bad guy for saying this—I no longer do follow-for-follow. I go to social media for escape. Yes, I follow my fellow local authors to support. Otherwise, I simply don't follow those whose posts I do not want showing up in my feed.

The other reason is this: I was shocked at how many of these so-called "supportive" authors unfollow you later. Yes, they got what they wanted from you, and later they go back and unfollow you.

There are apps you can download to see who has unfollowed you. It's often heartbreaking. I try not to use them anymore. I also just make sure those I follow are ones I want to see, even if they're not following me back.

Plus, let's be honest: most authors are not buying your books. They want to add to their follower count and find people who will retweet about their books. Following other authors is good when it comes to learning more about writing, motivation, publishing, and general industry stuff, but it's not going to help you sell books.

The success stories I've seen on Twitter are simple: follow and interact with those who share similar interests—people who love horror, for example, and are not all horror authors. Be genuine in your posts and share your passions. Then, occasionally, when you do tweet about your book, your followers are much more likely to engage with that post.

Social media can be toxic, self-serving, and overwhelming.

Let's do our part to build real community.

Like Instagram, you can find a community of supportive writers on Twitter using certain tags—most notably (at the time of this publication) #amwriting and #writingcommunity are often trending.

Similar to Instagram, there's a huge follow-for-follow community. I've found genuinely supportive authors that way, but as I cautioned above—I would be sure they are ones you would want to follow.

The best way to find support on Twitter is through consistent and genuine interaction. Retweet people. Tag them on #FF (Follow Friday). The more you do that, the more support you will, in turn, find. It can be a lot of work—all of social media is, really.

My advice is to play with the big three—Facebook, Instagram, and Twitter—for a year. See where you get the most interaction, then as you move forward, you can devote more time to the platform that works best for you. After all, we need to have time to write, and it's hard to always be online.

You can also do paid advertising with Twitter, which is fun and different from Facebook. On Twitter, you can target an individual's followers, so I can pay to have a tweet seen by those who follow Stephen King. It's just another avenue worth exploring!


GOODREADS


If you're not already on Goodreads, go create an account right now!

You're a reader, aren't you? Goodreads is the social media platform for reading and reviewing books! Confession: I didn't genuinely start using it until January 2019. But I love it.

When I start a book, I scan it using my Goodreads app or enter it manually as "currently reading."

When I finish the book, I give it a rating and a brief review. I copy my review and often post it (with a picture of the book) on my other social media accounts (using appropriate tags on Twitter and Instagram).

This is one way of gaining some followers who like book recommendations. I figure that doing this consistently over the years will help when it's time for me to release a new book, the goal being that anyone who follows me on Goodreads and other social media accounts will see my new release.

Goodreads is also a way to help support your fellow authors. You can add their books as "want to read" on your account. You can share your Goodreads profile on your other social media platforms too to gain followers.

Also, when you do have a book come out, you want to encourage people to add it on Goodreads. You want all the exposure you can get. Having all your friends, family, and social media followers add your book on Goodreads is a must! Then, encourage them to rate it at the very least, and politely ask for reviews, too.

When I search for a new read at a bookstore, I always look at its rating on Goodreads. It helps a potential future reader make a decision on whether or not to purchase your book.

When you have a book available, you can also run a Goodreads giveaway. You only need to have one book available, but you set this up as a contest. This is a great way to have readers add your book to their "to be read" list. Most winners are also great about leaving reviews, too.

The tips when running a giveaway are similar to running an ad. Have a concise, fun description of your book, a great cover, and mail books promptly to winners. You can share your giveaway link on your social media accounts also.

When you're ready to start a giveaway, go here: https://www.goodreads.com/giveaway/show_create_options

## PAID ADVERTISING

In addition to Facebook/Instragram and Twitter, you can also get paid advertising on Reddit, Amazon, and Goodreads. My recommendation is to create a monthly advertising budget. Spend that budget all in one place each month. Keep track of sales. What's working the best for you?

So, one month spend some money on Facebook ads. The next, Twitter. The next, Goodreads. The next, Amazon. And so on. Track your monthly sales, and return to the platforms where you have had the most success.

BookBub is another popular site for paid advertising. It's worth exploring as yet another possible avenue for selling your books. To see what it's all about, start here: https://www.bookbub.com/partners/boost_sales_and_visibility

Yes, this can get expensive, especially if you are not selling books. Pull money and stop ad campaigns if you are not selling. Rethink your strategy, how you are describing your book, and don't be afraid to ask others for help. You may be great at writing a novel, but you can still ask for help in writing those ads.


## BLOGS

Using Wordpress or Blogger, many authors try to write blog posts. I know some who post weekly or biweekly—little reflections on life, personal stories, whatever. This can be a great way to get your name out there and stay relevant in between books.

I find it to be a lot of work, especially when I'm already trying to find time to write my next book.

But in the months leading up to a book release, blogging can be another way to find your audience. I created a blog and posted weekly articles, everything from my writing advice, to book reviews, to teasers about my book, to stories about my dog or personal stuff—whatever I think someone may be interested in reading. Currently, I have done a horrible job keeping up with it. I perhaps post one or two articles a year on there. But I did find it to be a useful tool to generate excitement before a release.


## AMAZON

The challenge with Amazon is that they are constantly changing. They used to offer giveaways, where you could buy copies of your ebook and do contests on Amazon. As of the time of this writing, that's gone (so use Goodreads).

You can do paid promotions through your Amazon KDP page. (Click "promote and advertise.")

With Amazon, I would focus primarily on one thing: Get your readers to post reviews and ratings. Like Goodreads, your ratings are a way of building buyer confidence in your books. At local events, I have had readers pull my books up on Amazon just to see what the reviews are.

And getting people to post reviews isn't easy. I probably have one review for every one-thousand books sold. It can take a lot of effort, but it's worth your time and energy.

On my social media accounts, I encourage people to please post a review, reminding them how important it can be for a new author. In person with friends and family, I am not shy about this— "Hey, when you have time, do you mind leaving a review? Even just one sentence helps!"

Now, be careful. Amazon is constantly cracking down on what it considers to be fake reviews. More than one review from the same household may get all reviews from that household taken down. I've even heard things that if you're Facebook friends with the reviewer, Amazon may not allow the review, as they think it could be biased. I've still had luck with Facebook friends posting reviews, though.

The best option is to make sure they purchased the book on Amazon so that they get a "verified purchase" badge on the review. I like to hold contests on my pages—"friends, I'm giving away a $20 Amazon gift card! To enter, all you have to do is leave an honest review of my book. Every review this month will be entered into a drawing! This really helps me out, and this is my way of thanking you. Please review!"

Whenever someone tells me they liked my book, I thank them and then say, "Did you leave a review online? Gosh, I'd really appreciate if you could do that."

Be kind but persistent here, and work to get several ratings and reviews.

And don't be bothered by negative reviews. We'll talk about that a bit in a later chapter/

WEBSITE/NEWSLETTER

As you grow your platform, you may want to create a website. I use wix.com and you can view how I've set my website up at https://www.joechianakas.com/

Wix gives you free templates, and you can pay to have an upgraded site. You have to buy a domain name and renew that every year (I use GoDaddy.com to buy my domain of joechianakas.com).

It's a good place to direct readers who don't use social media. I also created a newsletter that I have on my site. I use MailChimp.com, which gives you a free subscription newsletter (at least free until you reach a massive number of subscribers, and if you get that many, it will be worth paying for it)!

I use my newsletter mainly to post new release announcements along with specials and sales. This is something I would work on, if you plan on having more than one book published.

Lots of authors really promote their newsletters. I've seen two main strategies. First, authors do newsletter takeovers, especially once you've accumulated several subscribers. That means you basically swap—one author lets you post your book and send out news to all their subscribers, if in turn you will do the same. The second strategy I see for building followers is to give away a free digital download to anyone who subscribes to your newsletter. You could send a PDF copy via email to all subscribers. Or you could use programs like BookFunnel. BookFunnel is another author support tool designed to help you grow newsletter subscribers and followers. There's a small fee for first-time authors, but this may be another source worth exploring to promote your books. Go to: https://bookfunnel.com/

Browse my website for some ideas. Also, look up your favorite author's website. What does he/she have online? I would also look at your favorite authors on the other social media platforms you use. You can get many good ideas just by doing that!

THINK OUTSIDE THE BOX

My success with *Rabbit in Red* came because of the old "think outside the box" mentality. There are thousands of books in bookstores, and hundreds-of-thousands of books available online. The more you dive into this world, the more you are going to feel that everyone has a book published these days. At one point, I started thinking that there may be more writers than readers—no joke!

How does one compete with that?

In my opinion, you get creative. It goes back to a couple questions we've discussed in previous chapters.

Where is my audience? How can I reach them?

My idea was to contact pop culture subscription boxes— monthly mystery boxes sent to pop culture-loving fans. Would my book be a good fit? I thought so.

For those boxes who thought the book would be too heavy and cost too much in shipping, we printed postcard-sized covers that I signed, which included digital download codes on the back (note: digital download codes are easy to get using Smashwords for ebooks, if you upload your digital book to that platform; Amazon does not have this option available, at this time).

I'm not saying copy me.

I'm saying copy the way I was thinking.

Where is your audience for your particular book? How can you reach them?

PRESS RELEASES

Traditionally, local media is a good place to contact for book releases, especially if you are having a book signing at a local business. Write up an announcement that features information about you, your book, and the event. The more unique you can make it, the better. For example, if it's your first book, say that. If you work in the community, include that, too. "Local teacher publishes first book . . ."

You'll have the best luck at small, community papers. The bigger papers and local news are harder these days, as content like this is often paid for. Local news features its advertisers. That doesn't mean it's not worth trying! Perhaps you can discuss this with the store where you are doing the event. They likely have some experience contacting local media.

One big tip, in general, for book releases—find online news sites and social media pages to submit your book release information to as well. This would be more for the online release, and not a local event.

I keep my eye out for entertainment blogs, particularly those that do reviews and articles related to my genre. I will send those writers press releases or ask them if they'd be willing to do a review. I've had luck with some pretty big online blogs and websites (as well as their social media accounts). Again, this may be the answer to the question, "Where is my audience?" I ask myself what my ideal audience is consuming online and what pages they follow. Then I try to contact those resources. It may take a dozen pitches before one says yes, but this is something I would definitely work on.

It also helps to be a fan of these pages. If you can genuinely say, "I'm a fan and I follow your page …" then add your book release info followed by why their readers may like it and how appreciative you would be, then you're on the right track.

STREET TEAM

This is one of my favorite ways to help get the word out for my books, but it certainly requires having a very supportive network. When I'm getting ready for a release, I post something like the following on my social media pages: "Friends! I am organizing a 'street team' for the upcoming release of my book. This is a fun group that helps post about the release, in exchange for fun prizes like Amazon gift cards and of course my eternal gratitude. Please message if you are willing to help. I can use all the help I can get!"

Then, what do you do with your street team? Here are some of the activities I've had them do.

First. I have them share my author page and ask them to invite their friends to like it. Currently, Facebook notifies you when a friend has accepted your invite to like a page. So, I give my team a three day deadline or so, and the person who gets the page the most likes earns a gift card! (You have to decide how much this is worth, as we'll potentially be doing a lot of challenges. I would say at least ten bucks.)

When the book comes out, I ask them all to buy it. I keep the ebook cheap, and I tell them that if it's a financial issue, then I will of course buy it for them. But I am honest and tell them that I have a lot of expenses involved with the release, and I'm hoping they wanted to read it anyway.

Just as important, and why I am having them buy it, is to get started posting reviews. I have them post reviews on Amazon and Goodreads. I give examples (guys—reviews can be just a sentence or two—"What an exciting story of suspense, I couldn't put it down") and then do another prize. Everyone who has posted a review by a certain date is entered for the next gift card!

What else could you have them do? Have them share their reviews. Have them take pics reading it and posting it. Have them help you develop advertising taglines. Ask for their ideas.

When I have the street team created, I make a private Facebook group where I can message them all of this.

Most importantly, express your constant gratitude for their help. And be willing to return the favor.


## BE YOU, BE REAL, BE PERSISTENT BUT NOT AGGRESSIVE

Once you start following other authors, you'll learn other ideas. There's no limit on marketing, and you really need to be promoting your work regularly (and not feel bad for doing so!). Who else is going to promote your work?

With that said, I don't post about my books every day on my personal social media accounts.

Here are a few other things I avoid:

1. Don't set up automatic direct messaging. This is a sure way to annoy people from the first second they start to follow you.

2. Don't waste your energy joining author groups trying to be the next "Bestselling USA Today author." It's a silly trend that authors do. They join forces with dozens if not hundreds of authors and get everyone they know to buy some kind of anthology book just to claim to be a bestseller. A much better use of your time is to focus on good writing and genuine marketing.

3. Don't make every post about writing or word count or how much you suffer as a writer. It gets old quick.

4. Be positive. Be real. Be you.

## UNFOLLOWERS

I mentioned before that you can find unfollower apps. They are slow and come with lots of ads. But you can search your phone's app store if this interests you. What they do: They show you who has unfollowed you on social media, so that you can unfollow them.

Again, if you follow those that genuinely interest you, and you strive to build an authentic social media platform, then you shouldn't even have to worry about this.

## WRITER'S DIGEST

Pick up a copy of *Writer's Digest* (a monthly magazine with great tips!). Barnes & Noble carries copies. You can check with your local library, too. I would read every issue to get tips on agents, writing, querying, and marketing.

## NETGALLEY

Another opportunity—although an expensive one if you are self-published—is Netgalley. In short, Netgalley allows you to feature your work to reviewers and influencers in the book industry. You pay to be featured and to have your work promoted, but this is a way for bloggers, educators, librarians, the media and more to discover your book. I have not tried this yet, but it's on my list of things to eventually do, which is why I am previewing it here for you.

Go to https://www.netgalley.com/

Specifically, browse the information for "publishers and authors."

## ETSY/PAYPAL/EBAY

I also recommend authors make signed copies available for purchase! You potentially can make more profit this way than by selling paperbacks off Amazon (order at the wholesale price and selling them directly for retail will often give you the biggest profit margin). Plus, sites like Etsy allow you to enter your product and keywords for your product, so it's another way to promote your work. I offer holiday deals on Etsy, and they help you set up shipping and everything. Similarly, you could use PayPal or Ebay.

Here's my Etsy shop if you want to take a look and get ideas: https://www.etsy.com/shop/FrightFest4D

## SUMMARY

This is the longest chapter in this short book. It's because when I first started writing, I never knew that I'd have to market my book, too. I thought I'd have a publisher who would do that for me.

This is what you have to do if you want to sell books, even if you have an agent and publisher.

These ideas are just the beginning. I encourage you to re-read this chapter as often as you can, writing notes on new ideas as you go, and never being afraid to take a risk.

Remember that advertising is a process. Maybe you don't sell ten books on the day you run an ad or set up a series of posts. But if you run ads and create posts and employ these ideas consistently over time, you will sell books. Maybe not thousands. But you will sell some.

You're a creative writer, right? Use some of that creativity in your marketing too!

# 18

# Getting and Dealing with Reviews

As mentioned in the marketing chapter with the Amazon and Goodreads sections, you want to strive for as many reviews as you can. It helps to post on social media—asking for honest reviews. But what I found most useful is just directly messaging and directly asking people who I know bought and read the book to post an honest review.

Don't ask anyone to lie for you or say they liked the book when they didn't.

It helps to have a strong foundation of reviews because readers do look these up, and they'll have more confidence in purchasing your book if you have some good reviews.

However, you shouldn't strive for perfection. A flag goes way up whenever I see a book with nothing but five-star reviews. Not even *Harry Potter* has all five-star reviews! If your book receives a balance of reviews, that's a good thing. Of course, you want more five-star and four-star reviews than you want one-star reviews, but some bad reviews actually help.

I look at it this way: you're not a real author until you've received some negative reviews!

I still remember my first one-star review. My heart was broken because I knew the person who wrote the review, too. I was invited by a local librarian to be a guest at a book club. Her book club had chosen my book for their October read. "Would you be willing to come as our guest and talk to us about your book?" she asked. It was my first book club invite, and I was so excited! I made bookmarks and brought some thank-you gifts. We talked about the book, and it was a pleasant discussion. Later I checked Goodreads, and I saw that the same local librarian who invited me and selected my book for her club was the very first person to leave me a one-star review.

Even worse, she wrote, "I don't like horror" as her review. Then why would you even choose my book? Why invite me?

Oh, it bothers me to this day, if you can't tell.

Since then, I've been fortunate—yes, fortunate!—to have received several other one-star and two-star reviews. It adds a layer of authenticity to my reviews. I'm also fortunate to have more four-star and five-star reviews than I do those bad ones. It's the balance that helps paint a good picture. Readers who do like horror may see that librarian's review and think, "Well I like this genre, so that doesn't bother me."

As you accumulate reviews, you can use them in a variety of ways. First, I take excerpts of the good reviews and use them as marketing quotes. One reader called my book, "The Hogwarts of Horror." I've used that line in several marketing posts. Second, when you send out press releases to entertainment sites or local news, you can also quote some of the reviews. Third, when you "think outside the box" and ask yourself where your readers are (unique local business, subscription boxes, etc), you may want to direct those businesses to your reviews and tell them to not just take your word for it, but to see what readers have been saying. I do the same thing if I pitch my book to any book clubs (of course, I make sure they actually enjoy horror if I'm pitching *Rabbit in Red*!).

Now, with all that said, let me tell you this: you have to get to a point where you stop checking your reviews. It can drive you crazy.

I wanted one-hundred reviews in one year. That's hard to achieve, just so you know! You may start with a goal of ten reviews per month, and then modify your expectations a bit based on what you are able to accomplish. Again, go back to marketing—think of how a street team can help, or do some general contests/giveaways for people who post reviews, and don't be afraid to ask people directly. "Hey, long story short, but I'm trying to get to fifty reviews for marketing purposes. I know you picked up my book and THANK YOU for that. Would you mind going to Amazon and/or Goodreads and just leaving a short review? Even just a sentence or two. Here are the links . . ." That's what made the biggest difference for me.

If you look up my reviews, you'll notice that book one of *Rabbit in Red* has a lot of reviews, and the other two books in my series do not. That's because I did not employ these strategies with book two or book three. There are two reasons for that. First, I really did work hard to get over one-hundred reviews of book one, and it took a lot of persistent posting and messaging. Quite simply, I wasn't going to bother people again. If they left a review for the other books in the series, great. If not, that's okay. Because reason two: for a series, I need the most reviews for book one so that people start it. That's the biggest goal. So, with all that said, be persistent but not annoying, and always be grateful.

Also, never respond to reviews, especially negative ones. That's unprofessional.

My general advice is this:

I leave reviews for the books I read on Goodreads. Model the kind of reviews you would want. I never try to be super negative or show how smart I think I am by picking apart a story. If I don't like a story, I say very little, or I don't even leave a review. There's enough negativity in the world.

Get to the point where you don't read your negative reviews. It's hard not to, and again you have to realize that if you are to sell books and be successful, then you will get some negative reviews! But train yourself to just stop checking, eventually.

Don't change how you write because of a reader review. Make sure you have a good reading team and editor to rely on.

Remember—you wrote a book, and that's something to celebrate. There will always be haters and negative people, especially online. If you must dwell on that (again, please think of every possible strategy you can to not even look at the bad reviews), then use it as fuel to write the next best book you can. Just keep writing.

# 19

## Am I Ready To Publish?

One of the biggest questions writers ask is, "How do I know when I'm ready to publish?" I wish there was an easy answer for this question.

I have always looked at it in terms of this: when your talent meets your passion, you're ready.

In other words—and forgive me for generalizing young writers—I meet many teenagers and young adults who have a great passion for writing. They have a great story idea. They might even be able to sit at a computer and crank out 70,000 words.

Has their talent, though, caught up with their passion?

I know I'm generalizing, so again forgive me, but when I was twenty-two, I know I sure didn't have the writing talent to publish an entire novel. I actually did write a full young adult book (65,000 words) at twenty-two. Not a single soul on Earth has ever read it. It was an exercise more in discipline (to see if I could write a full story from beginning to end). The writing was not good. It's not something I would want to share with the world.

Of course, there are exceptions to the rule—a sixteen-year-old with great talent who deserves to find a publisher, for example. With the ease of self-publishing, though, I give lots of credit to those who ask this question, "Am I ready to publish?"

The only ways to get better at writing are to keep reading and keep writing. Read a book a week, or at least a book a month, if you're busy with work and/or school. Practice writing with short stories. Keep a great journal—physical or online—with story ideas.

This isn't to say my *Rabbit in Red* book is amazing, but here's an example: What if the idea for that book came to me at seventeen and I tried to write it then? Would it be as good?

Doubtful, right? So, sometimes our talent has to catch up with our passion, and we owe it to ourselves to keep developing our talent through lots of reading and writing.

Okay, so let's say you have a novel fully written or some kind of book (at any age) and you ask the question, "How do I know when it's ready?"

This is when I would rely on a team of readers. It all goes back to revising and editing. I really hope you don't go immediately from writing a book to publishing without a thorough revision process with a team of readers. Even if you are incredibly talented, that revision process will make your work even better. Even Stephen King still has a reading team and editors to this day.

Many writers rely on close friends, a partner, or family to be their readers, and that's fine—but I challenge this: Will they be 100% honest with you? Are you asking them to be 100% honest with you?

Your goal, in answering this question, is to take your work to someone who can be fully honest with you. Someone who can answer the question with a "not yet, but you're close." I know the answer we want to hear is a resounding "Yes!"

You'll get there, if you're willing to put in the work revising the book and having people tell you "you're close." That's a great sign.

Go back to the writing process chapters earlier in this book. Write your book. Put it away for a month. Re-read and revise. Give it to readers. Get feedback. Revise again. Get an editor. Revise again.

If you have done all that, ask your team, "Am I ready?"

I'll bet you'll get that "yes!"

And I bet you'll find the confidence in yourself to be able to say "yes" also. The more work you put into revising and getting feedback, the more confidence you will have with yourself. And guess what—that's also how your talent catches up with your passion. You owe it to your story to make sure you have given it your best.

*Disclaimer*: Next to the question, "How did you publish your book?" the biggest question I get is, "Will you read my book and tell me what you think?"

I'm sorry, but I can't. I get this question at least once a week. I would spend all of my time reading other people's work and not have nearly enough time to work on my own.

Here's what I will tell you: When your book is published, send me the links. I will add it to my "to be read" Goodreads links.

I'm not an editor. I know how hard it can be to find a good reader and editor. I'm sorry, but I can't be that person for you. You have to learn to say no sometimes, and you have to find your own people to help you with that part of this journey.

In the future, I'd love to do fundraisers or something for charity—one where everyone who donates gets entered to win a free reading critique that I would be willing to do. But please understand how time-consuming that is, and I just have to say no to individual requests in order to maintain my own work-life balance.

I would encourage you to find honest readers with strong opinions, preferably ones who are not also super busy working on their own books. That's your best bet.

# 20

# Audiobooks and Narrating Opportunities

Once you self-publish your book, you may want to consider creating an audiobook. A site definitely worth exploring is https://www.acx.com/

ACX allows you to do multiple things. You can submit your manuscript and hire a narrator. You can upload your own audio. Plus, you can audition for jobs narrating other author's books.

Hiring a narrator is a pretty simple process through ACX. You simply upload a sample of your manuscript, and narrators will record themselves reading that sample. You get to listen to the auditions and choose who would like. ACX creates a contract between you and the narrator you hire. The contract splits royalties of audiobook sales between you and the narrator, and of course ACX gets a portion of every sale too.

This is another way to reach readers with little work on your end, as someone else does the narration and ACX does all the legal work and payroll.

If you have your own audio recording equipment and want to record your own book, then you can also use ACX to upload your own manuscript. You wouldn't share royalties with anyone, but ACX still gets its share.

ACX distributes books to Audible, iTunes, and Amazon. Your audiobook will be available on the biggest audiobook platforms!

In addition, if you are looking for extra job opportunities and have good audio recording equipment, you can review narration opportunities. I don't think, with rare exception, anyone makes a lot of money from being a narrator (it all depends on sales), but if you enjoy reading out loud, it could be a good opportunity.

# 21

# Digital Platforms for Authors

In today's digital medium, there are several ways to build your audience and improve your writing.

RADISH

Explore https://www.radishfiction.com/

WATTPAD

Explore https://www.wattpad.com/

TAPAS

Explore https://tapas.io/

On one hand, this is a way to practice your writing one episode or chapter at a time while getting reader feedback. You can publish full novels, but most of these allow (or feature) bite-sized reading. If you're just starting out and are a new writer, I would recommend playing with any of these sites. It's a digital way of getting those readers and that essential feedback. If you already have some experience, you can also submit work—if appropriate to what they feature—and make money, too.

For example, I use Tapas as another avenue for my digital work. I submitted my content and was offered a premium contract, which means my work gets featured and I get paid for it, as readers have to buy the content. Like many of these apps and sites, they break the novel into Snapchat size "episodes" instead of chapters (about 1000 words per episode). Readers pay just pennies, typically, for each episode, but if they read the entire book, they will have spent a few dollars.

It doesn't sound like much, but I've profited very well from Tapas when I have a new release that fits with the type of content their readers consume (remember to ask—who are my readers and where are they?).

But if you don't get a contract or a paid deal with these sites, remember that it's also a good place to start writing and to build that audience. Over time, your writing will improve, and you will learn to find the digital platforms that match the kind of work you enjoy creating. Unlike Amazon, these are very interactive platforms. Once you find readers, you likely may have multiple comments and reader discussion on each episode. Plus, you can interact with them, too! (Remember never to react poorly to a bad review, though.) Authors who engage with their audiences on these platforms tend to be more successful. Plus, several authors have been picked up by the big publishers, all because their work was successful on one of these digital platforms.

Keep in mind that if you publish on these sites, you should not be exclusive on Amazon and not enroll your book in Kindle Unlimited. Also, make sure you understand the rules of each of these sites. They vary. They may want your work to be exclusive with them—if you are getting paid—for a set amount of time before you would self-publish the content on Amazon.

I would simply browse the websites and see if what these platforms feature match the kind of writing you do. Read some of the featured work. Get a feel for it, and trust your instincts.

It's entirely possible, trust me, that your work could do much better on one of these platforms than on Amazon.

# 23
# My Publishing Story

My publishing journey has been wild, to say the least, and I don't mean wild in a good way. It's been difficult and challenging. I've considered giving up dozens of times. I've asked myself, "Why do you do this when it causes so much stress?" I share that with you because it's important to know what you're in for. Yes, there are joys, but let me share with you my story.

When I first wrote *Rabbit in Red* (what would become my first published novel), I dreamed that it would be the next *Harry Potter*. Foolish, I know. I got the idea for *Rabbit in Red* on a hot, summer afternoon while reading another book in my back yard. I outlined my novel that day. I started writing the next day. In three weeks of obsessive passion, I completed a 70,000-word manuscript.

(I have never written anything so quickly or feverishly since then, by the way. But we will get to that.)

I gave it a quick read for typos and minor edits, and then I excitedly queried the biggest known agents I could find.

Predictable spoiler coming: It got rejected.

What I learned is that we must let our passions cool down. We must step far enough away from our work to see it in a different perspective. I let myself cool for a couple months, and then I reread and rewrote the 70,000-word manuscript. Then I took it to close friends who were good, critical readers, and I asked for honest feedback. "Tear it apart!" I said.

And they did. I fell into a dark sadness for a good day or two. I thought about their feedback, and I revised the entire manuscript again. This time, when I sent it to agents and publishers, I started getting some bites.

I learned right then and there that the key to writing is revising. And the key to revising is finding good, critical readers.

Several agents requested full manuscripts. That's a huge step, and that's your goal. You'll rarely (and probably never) send someone a full manuscript immediately. Agents want to read a one-page query and a few pages of your book. That's all they have time for, as they receive hundreds of queries. So, it's very promising to get a full manuscript request. It means your premise has promise and your writing has potential! (Celebrate full requests, always!)

One New York City agent who also is a film scout for a major TV network requested a full from me. She rejected it, but in one email wrote, "This would make a great TV show, and I considered proposing it to the network. But then when (a certain part of the novel happened), I knew it wouldn't work."

Wow. What a compliment and rejection all at once. But it fired me up and gave me hope to keep working. Finally, on a Superbowl Sunday, I received an email from a small publisher that read, "We would like to offer you a contract for *Rabbit in Red*, and we cannot wait to get your book out to the world."

I did my reference checks on the publisher. There was nothing promising, honestly, but I had no other great options. So, I signed with them.

And they were terrible. It was the worst experience of my life. Heart-breaking, dream-crushing. I could write a book on that experience, but I won't. Here's the truth: One person led a "publishing" company out of her bedroom, with a few other authors on board to help. They didn't proofread, they didn't have any real marketing skills, and the publisher often went MIA for weeks at a time and couldn't be reached.

They published book one of *Rabbit in Red* with so many formatting errors and typos that it made me more embarrassed than I could possibly tell you. How can I ever come back from that? If that was my first impression to friends and readers, then crap. I'm done.

Luckily, they closed their doors and went out of business. Shocker, I know. Rights came back to me. I kept *Rabbit in Red* as a self-published book, and my new mission was to make it successful on my own. Everything I learned since then is what, in fact, I'm trying to put in this book—tips so you can do this on your own and advice to at least hopefully prevent embarrassing deals like I experienced.

While continuing to work on the rest of the trilogy, I brainstormed all sorts of publishing ideas. Who is my audience? Where are they? How do I stand out among millions of books?

For me, the idea came through pop culture subscription boxes. It was always a dream of mine to be included in Horror Block, a major company out of Canada (part of Nerd Block) who shipped quality pop culture items to thousands around the world. In the first chapter of *Rabbit in Red*, my main character collects Horror Blocks. During my phone call with the publisher that went out of business, I asked if she thought we could ever sell them the book. She laughed and said, "Anything's possible." Her tone implied, "Yeah, right."

But once I had the rights back to my own book, I pitched it to Horror Block. It took months to get a response, and I didn't ever give up. I didn't email them every day, but I reached out at least once a month, tagging them on Twitter, emailing staff, and so on. Then one summer day, a Horror Block representative called me. She said she loved the book and she asked . . .

Wait for it . . .

"How much for 16,000 copies?"

I passed out. I had sold a thousand or so on my own, and even that took a TON of work. (Most self-published authors are lucky to sell one-hundred copies of a book, to be honest. It's not any better, honestly, for those working with really small publishers.)

Horror Block shipped *Rabbit in Red* to thousands of people around the world, and suddenly I had an audience. From there, lots of pop culture subscription boxes picked it up. It's appeared in Box of Dread, Bam Horror, Spearcraft Book Box, BookLoot, and more. Some boxes created special editions. Some had signed copies. Over the course of a year, I signed at least 20,000 items for these various boxes. And Horror Block came back and picked up 10,000 copies of book two. Suddenly, I had fans and an audience!

It goes back to the basic questions: Who is my audience? Where are they? Obviously, I can't answer that for you, but those questions should lead you in the right direction.

And then guess what happened in my series of never-ending obstacles . . . Horror Block declared bankruptcy and went out of business.

See how hard this is? The doors to me easily selling thousands of copies of my novels closed.

Self-publishing is hard. You are constantly fighting for an audience in a world of hundreds of thousands of authors. I wanted a team to support me. That's why I went to a publisher in the first place. That's why I was so grateful to have partnered with Horror Block.

During that time, I also started working with a digital app called Tapas. They published my work there, and they helped me reach thousands of new readers, too. Thankfully (at the time of this writing), Tapas is doing very well. There are a lot of good digital apps that may be a resource for you depending on your genre.

Also during that time, I had been working on a new horror novel titled *Darkness Calls*. Tapas was helping me reach thousands of digital readers and paying great royalties, but I can't help but want those beautiful print editions. I still fight for the dream of my books appearing in every bookstore around the world.

Before they went out business, I was certain I could self-publish and get Horror Block to pick up another ten thousand copies. But now they closed down . . . so what do I do?

It was time to start over. I queried agents just like I did with the first *Rabbit in Red* book years ago. It took over a year and multiple revisions, all while working with an editor, following the same process as before (write, sit on it for a month or so, get readers, revise, etc). A year later, I had multiple agents request full manuscripts, and finally someone offered a contract of representation!

I made it, right?

Well, my agent picked up *Darkness Calls* in winter of 2019. She said she wanted to wait until fall 2019 to pitch it. Timing was everything. So, in the meantime, I wrote a different book, something not horror that would potentially reach a bigger demographic. It's a young adult contemporary novel called *Singlets and Secrets*.

Both *Darkness Calls* and *Singlets and Secrets* could easily have found great digital homes on Tapas. I could self-publish them in print, too. But my goal is to shoot for the stars.

When you are considering whether to self-publish or query agents, you have to ask yourself how patient you are and how long you are willing to wait. I told myself that I found success with *Rabbit in Red*, so why not be patient for a couple years and see what can happen? But if you don't want to wait, well . . . that's when self-publishing becomes a much more appealing option.

What else is interesting to me is that I worked on *Darkness Calls* for a good couple years. I hired my *Rabbit in Red* editor. I had multiple teams of people critique and edit before and after that. Years of work, really. It's my more "epic" story—dark, deep, bigger than anything. My agent compared it to Stephen King's IT, and I couldn't think of a better compliment. But I was still waiting for her to even pitch the book, so in the meantime, I wrote something different. I wanted to get outside of horror, and I have other passions.

*Singlets and Secrets* is a young adult story that has something for everyone, I think. Romance, action, suspense, big issues from bullying to LGBTQ diversity. And when my agent read it, she called it "wonderful." Now, guess what happened?

We put *Darkness Calls*, the book I poured my soul into for years, on the back burner. Instead, we are pitching *Singlets and Secrets* to publishers. At the time of this writing, several big and life-changing publishers have requested full manuscripts from her. But no one has made an offer.

And it's been months.

You see, this journey is tough. I wake up and wonder, "Will this be the day my book gets picked up?" I have two finished novels. Two other works-in-progress (because the only thing that really keeps me from going crazy thinking about all this is just to keep writing new stories).

In minutes, I could self-publish these and make them live to the world. But I choose, for now, to wait. To dream. To hope.

Patience is the most important characteristic to have, should you choose to pursue agents and publishers.

When (yes, WHEN not IF—it's all about confidence!), my books get picked up, it will likely be another year before they hit shelves. I'll work with a new editor. We'll revise them all over again. Release dates will be set well into the future.

So, a book I wrote in 2016 may very well not even see life until 2022.

But will it be a better book because I was patient and kept revising? Yes—that's what I tell myself at least. On the other hand, sometimes it would be nice to simply publish a book whenever I wanted. That's the perk of self-publishing (but also the perk of finding a strong, legitimate publisher that you may be able to work with for life!).

So, that's my publishing story so far in a nutshell. Everyone has different experiences, of course, so don't take this as the norm. Just keep an open mind, ask yourself good questions, and find a way to be equally persistent and patient, no matter what direction you choose.

I believe I will be successful. Because I believe that, I do whatever I can to succeed. It's not about one book. I'll write several until I create the right one to sell. It's not about one publisher. I may have to go through many until I find the best one for me.

If you believe in yourself, you're sure more likely to achieve your goals. So, even though I shared a lot of challenges and obstacles, I hope you'll stay positive, too.

Enjoy the journey, and just keep on writing.

December 26, 2019
Joe Chianakas

# Appendix:

## My checklist for self-publishing this book

I thought it might help to offer a final, concise checklist of what I did when writing and publishing this book. This is for print-on-demand, but use steps one through ten for ebooks as well.

_____ 1. Write the book :) ALSO, write the back-of-the-book blurb (summary/teaser) so that it's ready to go.

_____ 2. Set up formatting: For this book, I used page size 6 x 9; Margins set up as MIRRORED and labeled as Top: 0.94, Bottom: 0.94, Inside 0.9, Outside: 0.6

_____ 3. No tabs used; line spacing options via "Line and Paragraph Spacing" used instead.

_____ 4. Page breaks inserted in between chapters

_____ 5. Dedication and copyright page included; also check to see if you inserted page numbers and headers for your name/book title if you want headers.

_____ 6. Table of contents section added with page numbers (not applicable to fiction, but this is good for non-fiction or short story anthology).

_____ 7. Book saved to my computer and backed up on a flash drive (always save multiple places!).

____ 8. Do a final proofread (for most books of course, be sure to go through the full revision process as listed in chapters 6 and 7).

(The following is for print-on-demand via Amazon so that I do not have to pay for an ISBN and can self-publish with very little cost! Ingram will require you to purchase your own ISBN.)

____ 9. Create account or sign in to kdp.amazon.com

____ 10. Set up taxes and bank account info as needed so you get paid.

____ 11. Click "add new paperback." Follow the set up to add title, author, back-of-the-book blurb, and so on.

____ 12. Get free ISBN from Amazon. (Note for ebooks: Set DRM at "no", that's digital rights management.)

____ 13. For print, have book saved as a PDF. (For Kindle ebook, have it saved as a Word Doc.)

____ 14. Have your cover already created and saved as PDF, or use Amazon's cover creator.

____ 15. Enter appropriate keywords for people who would search for your book.

____ 16. Select two categories for your book.

____ 17. Select paper and cover type (for nonfiction—white interior; glossy cover; for fiction—cream interior, matte cover).

____ 17. Set pricing.

____ 18. Publish! (*Note: Get a proof copy mailed to you first and double-check everything before making it available publicly.*)

____ 19. Claim book on Amazon Author Central.

____ 20. Promote and celebrate!

Made in the USA
Monee, IL
05 January 2020